D1132607

WHAT MAKES A LEADER: LEADER:

WHY EMOTIONAL INTELLIGENCE MATTERS

DANIEL GOLEMAN

www.morethansound.net

What Makes a Leader: Why Emotional
Intelligence Matters / Daniel Goleman

1st Edition

ISBN 978-1-934441-74-9

Also by Daniel Goleman from More Than Sound

Leadership: A Master Class DVD series: with Bill George, Warren Bennis, George Kohlrieser and more

Leadership: The Power of Emotional Intelligence: Selected Writings

The Brain and Emotional Intelligence: New Insights

Better Parents, Better Spouses, Better People with Daniel Siegel

Knowing Our Emotions, Improving Our World with Paul Ekman

Training the Brain: Cultivating Emotional Intelligence with Richard Davidson

Good Work: Aligning Skills and Values with Howard Gardner

The Inner Compass for Ethics and Excellence with Naomi Wolf

Socially Intelligent Computing with Clay Shirky

Rethinking Education with George Lucas

Leading the Necessary Revolution with Peter Senge

Available at morethansound.net

WHAT MAKES A LEADER: WHY EMOTIONAL INTELLIGENCE MATTERS

INTRODUCTION

Which matters more for leadership that gets results: IQ or EQ? The paradox is that they both matter, but in very different ways.

There is no doubt that given a large population pool, IQ is the best way to sort people into which career they can handle: it takes an IQ about a standard deviation (an IQ of 115) to handle the cognitive complexity of professions like medicine or law, accounting or high-level executive.

But once people are in those roles, IQ drops away as a predictor of success. There is a "floor effect" for IQ – everyone else in those roles has been selected for a high IQ, and so they are all very smart. But when it comes to predicting who amongst those highly intelligent people will emerge as the most productive, the best team member or an outstanding leader, emotional intelligence increasingly matters.

That's because emotional intelligence skills – how well we manage ourselves and our relationships – are the skills that distinguish outstanding performers. And the higher one goes in an organization, the more EI matters in distinguishing the most effective leaders.

This collection of my writing on leadership and EI – mainly articles I've written in the *Harvard*

Business Review – reflects how my thinking has evolved. When I wrote *Emotional Intelligence* in the mid-1990s I included a short chapter, called "Managing with Heart," that made the simple argument that leaders need strengths in emotional intelligence. This, at the time, was a new and rather radical idea. That chapter, to my surprise, got lots of attention, particularly from people in management.

As I looked into the data on leadership and EI for my next book, *Working with Emotional Intelligence*, I became even more convinced. I took advantage of my training back in graduate school from David McClelland, who at the time was a pioneer in the method known as "competence modeling," which allows a systematic analysis of the specific strengths that make someone in a given role an outstanding performer. When I did a rough analysis of close to 200 such models from a wide range of organizations, I found that the large majority of competencies that distinguished the best leaders were based on EI, not IQ.

That caught the eye of editors at the *Harvard Business Review*, who asked me to write an article summarizing this. Called "What Makes a Leader," that article is the first chapter of this book. My next HBR article, "Leadership that Gets Results" – the second chapter here – summarized data from HayGroup on leadership styles that build on EI abilities, and their varying impacts on emotional climate of the organization.

As I looked more deeply at the new findings from neuroscience on the dynamics of relationships – and what that meant for the drivers of excellence and high-impact relationships – I again wrote for

HBR. Those articles, too, are included in this book.

My most recent thinking has shifted frameworks to explore how a leader's focus matters for effectiveness. The chapter "The Leader's Triple Focus" summarizes sections on leadership from my book *Focus: The Hidden Driver of Excellence*. And the final chapter, written for a magazine (by coincidence called *Focus*), published by Egon Zehnder International, reflects on the ethical dimension of leadership.

I've also included several of my blogs, placed after the relevant chapters, that either further delve into the topic or complement it. These first appeared, for the most part, on LinkedIn; some are from HBR.com.

I hope my reflections gathered here will help you along the way in your own leadership journey.

-Daniel Goleman
January, 2014

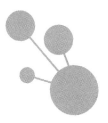

WHAT MAKES A LEADER?

Originally published in the Harvard Business Review, November/December 1998

Every businessperson knows a story about a highly intelligent, highly skilled executive who was promoted into a leadership position only to fail at the job. And they also know a story about someone with solid – but not extraordinary – intellectual abilities and technical skills who was promoted into a similar position and then soared. Such anecdotes support the widespread belief that identifying individuals with the "right stuff" to be leaders is more art than science. After all, the personal styles of superb leaders vary: Some leaders are subdued and analytical; others shout their manifestos from the mountaintops. And just as important, different situations call for different types of leadership. Most mergers need a sensitive negotiator at the helm, whereas many turnarounds require a more forceful authority. I have found, however, that the most effective leaders are alike in one crucial way: they all have a high degree of what has come to be known as emotional intelligence.

It's not that IQ and technical skills are irrelevant. They do matter, but mainly as "threshold capabilities"; that is, they are the entry-level requirements for executive positions. But my research, along with other recent studies, strongly suggests that emotional intelligence is the sine qua non of leadership. Without it, a person can have the best training in the world, an incisive, analytical mind, and an endless supply of smart ideas, but he still won't make a great leader. My colleagues and I have focused on how emotional intelligence operates at work. We have examined the relationship between emotional intelligence and effective performance, especially in leaders, and we have observed how emotional intelligence shows itself on the job. How can you tell if someone has high emotional intelligence, for example, and how can you recognize it in yourself? In the following pages, we'll explore these questions, taking each of the components of emotional intelligence – self-awareness, self-regulation, empathy, and social skill – in turn.

Most large companies today have employed trained psychologists to develop what are known as "competency models" to aid them in identifying, training, and promoting likely stars in the leadership firmament. The psychologists have also developed such models for lower-level positions. While writing *Working With Emotional Intelligence*, I analyzed competency models from 188 companies – most of which were large and global – as well as government agencies. In carrying out this work, my objective was to determine which personal capabilities drove outstanding performance within these organizations, and to what degree they did so. I grouped capabilities into three categories: purely technical skills like accounting and business planning; cognitive abilities like analytical reasoning; and competencies demonstrating emotional intelligence, such as the ability to work with others and effectiveness in leading change. To create some of the competency models, psychologists asked senior managers at the companies to identify the capabilities that typified the organization's most outstanding leaders. To create other models, the psychologists used objective criteria, such as a division's profitability, to differentiate the star performers at senior levels within their organizations from the average ones. Those individuals were then extensively interviewed and tested, and their capabilities were compared. This process resulted in the creation of lists of ingredients for highly effective leaders. The lists ranged in length from 7 to 15 items and included such ingredients as initiative and strategic vision. Some of the competencies reflected purely cognitive, IQ-type abilities, or purely technical skills, while others were based largely on emotional intelligence abilities like self-management.

When I analyzed all this data, I found dramatic results. To be sure, intellect was a driver of outstanding performance. Cognitive skills such as big-picture thinking and long-term vision were particularly important. But when I calculated the ratio of technical skills and IQ to emotional intelligence as ingredients of excellent performance, emotional intelligence proved to be twice as important as the others for jobs at all levels. Moreover, my analysis showed that emotional intelligence played an increasingly important role at the highest levels of the company, where differences in technical skills were of negligible importance.

In other words, the higher the rank of a person considered to be a star performer, the more emotional intelligence capabilities showed up as the reason for his or her effectiveness. When I compared star performers with average ones in senior leadership positions, nearly 90 percent of the competencies that distinguished outstanding performers were attributable to emotional intelligence factors, rather than purely cognitive abilities. Other researchers have confirmed that emotional intelligence not only distinguishes outstanding leaders, but can also be linked to strong performance.

The findings of the late David McClelland, the renowned researcher in human and organizational behavior, provide a good example. In a 1996 study of a global food and beverage company, McClelland found that when senior managers had a critical mass of emotional intelligence capabilities, their divisions outperformed yearly earnings goals by 20 percent. Meanwhile, division leaders without that critical mass underperformed by almost the same amount. McClelland's findings, interestingly, held as true in the company's U.S. divisions as in its divisions in Asia and Europe. In short, the numbers tell us a persuasive story about the link between a company's success and the emotional intelligence of its leaders. And just as important, research is also demonstrating that people can, if they take the right approach, develop their emotional intelligence.

SELF-AWARENESS

Self-awareness is the first component of emotional intelligence – which makes sense when one considers that the Delphic oracle gave the advice to "know thyself" thousands of years ago. Self-awareness means having a deep understanding of one's emotions, strengths, weaknesses, needs, and drives. People with strong self-awareness are neither overly critical nor unrealistically hopeful. Rather, they are honest with themselves and with others. People who have a high degree of self-awareness recognize how their feelings affect them, other people, and their job performance. Thus, a self-aware person who knows that tight deadlines bring out the worst in him plans his time carefully and gets his work done well in advance. Another person with high self-awareness will be able to work with a demanding client. She will understand the client's impact on her moods and the deeper reasons for her frustration. "Their trivial demands take us away from the real work that needs to be done," she might explain. And she will go one step further and turn her anger into something constructive.

Self-awareness extends to a person's understanding of his or her values and goals. Someone who is highly self-aware knows where he is headed and why; so, for example, he will be able to be firm in turning down a job offer that is tempting financially but does not fit with his principles or long-term goals. A person who lacks self-awareness is apt to make decisions that bring inner turmoil by treading on buried values. "The money looked good so I signed on," someone might say two years into a job, "but the work means so little to me that I'm constantly bored." The decisions of self-aware people mesh with their values; consequently, they often find work to be energizing.

How can one recognize self-awareness? First and foremost, it shows itself as candor and an ability to assess oneself realistically. People with high self-awareness are able to speak accurately and openly – although not necessarily effusively or confessionally – about their emotions and the impact they have on their work. For instance, one manager I know of was skeptical about a new personal-shopper service that her company, a major department-store chain, was about to introduce. Without prompting from her team or her boss, she offered them an explanation: "It's hard for me to get behind the rollout of this service," she admitted, "because I really wanted to run the project, but I wasn't selected. Bear with me while I deal with that." The manager did indeed examine her feelings; a week later, she was supporting the project fully. Such self-knowledge often shows itself in the hiring process. Ask a candidate to describe a time he got carried away by his feelings and did something he later regretted. Self-aware candidates will be frank in admitting to failure and will often tell their tales with a smile. One of the hallmarks of self-awareness is a self-deprecating sense of humor.

Self-awareness can also be identified during performance reviews. Self-aware people know and are comfortable talking about their limitations and strengths, and they often demonstrate a thirst for constructive criticism. By contrast, people with low self-awareness interpret the message that they need to improve as a threat or a sign of failure.

Self-aware people can also be recognized by their self-confidence. They have a firm grasp of their capabilities and are less likely to set themselves up to fail by, for example, overstretching on assignments. They know, too, when to ask for help. And the risks they take on the job are calculated. They won't ask for a challenge that they know they can't handle alone. They'll play to their strengths.

Consider the actions of a midlevel employee who was invited to sit in on a strategy meeting with her company's top executives. Although she was the most junior person in the room, she did not sit there quietly, listening in awestruck or fearful silence. She knew she had a head for clear logic and the skill to present ideas persuasively, and she offered cogent suggestions about the company's strategy. At the same time, her self-awareness stopped her from wandering into territory where she knew she was weak. Despite the value of having self-aware people in the workplace, my research indicates that senior executives don't often give self-awareness the credit it deserves when they look for potential leaders. Many executives mistake candor about feelings for "wimpiness" and fail to give due respect to employees who openly acknowledge their shortcomings. Such people are too readily dismissed as "not tough enough" to lead others.

In fact, the opposite is true. In the first place, people generally admire and respect candor. Furthermore, leaders are constantly required to make judgment calls that require a candid assessment of capabilities – their own and those of others. Do we have the management expertise to acquire a competitor? Can we launch a new product within six months? People who assess themselves honestly – that is, self-aware people – are well suited to do the same for the organizations they run.

SELF-MANAGEMENT

Biological impulses drive our emotions. We cannot do away with them, but we can do much to manage them. Self-regulation, which is like an ongoing inner conversation, is the component of emotional intelligence that frees us from being prisoners of our feelings. People engaged in such a conversation feel bad moods and emotional impulses just as everyone else does, but they find ways to control them and even to channel them in useful ways. Imagine an executive who has just watched a team of his employees present a botched analysis to the company's board of directors. In the gloom that follows, the executive might find himself tempted to pound on the table in anger or kick over a chair. He could leap up and scream at the group. Or he might maintain a grim silence, glaring at everyone before stalking off. But if he had a gift for self-regulation, he would choose a different approach. He would pick his words carefully, acknowledging the team's poor performance without rushing to any hasty judgment. He would then step back to consider the reasons for the failure. Are they personal – a lack of effort? Are there any mitigating factors? What was his role in the debacle? After considering these questions, he would call the team together, lay out the incident's consequences, and offer his feelings about it. He would then present his analysis of the problem and a well-considered solution.

Why does self-regulation matter so much for leaders? First of all, people who are in control of their feelings and impulses – that is, people who are reasonable – are able to create an environment of trust and fairness. In such an environment, politics and infighting are sharply reduced and productivity is high. Talented people flock to the organization and aren't tempted to leave. And self-regulation has a trickle-down effect. No one wants to be known as a hothead when the boss is known for her calm approach. Fewer bad moods at the top mean fewer throughout the organization. Second, self-regulation is important for competitive reasons. Everyone knows that business today is rife with ambiguity and change. Companies merge and break apart regularly. Technology transforms work at a dizzying pace. People who have mastered their emotions are able to roll with the changes. When a new program is announced, they don't panic; instead, they are able to suspend judgment, seek out information, and listen to the executives as they explain the new program. As the initiative moves forward, these people are able to move with it. Sometimes they even lead the way.

Consider the case of a manager at a large manufacturing company. Like her colleagues, she had used a certain software program for five years. The program drove how she collected and reported data and how she thought about the company's strategy. One day, senior executives announced that a new program was to be installed that would radically change how information was gathered and assessed within the organization. While many people in the company complained bitterly about how disruptive the change would be, the manager mulled over the reasons for the new program and was convinced of its potential to improve performance. She eagerly attended training sessions – some of her colleagues refused to do so – and was eventually promoted to run several divisions, in part because she used the new technology so effectively.

I want to push the importance of self-regulation to leadership even further and make the case that it enhances integrity, which is not only a personal virtue but also an organizational strength. Many of the bad things that happen in companies are a function of impulsive behavior. People rarely plan to exaggerate profits, pad expense accounts, dip into the till, or abuse power for selfish ends. Instead, an opportunity presents itself, and people with low impulse control just say yes. By contrast, consider the behavior of the senior executive at a large food company. This executive was scrupulously honest in his negotiations with local distributors. He would routinely lay out his cost structure in detail, thereby giving the distributors a realistic understanding of the company's pricing. This approach meant the executive couldn't always drive a hard bargain. Now, on occasion, he felt the urge to increase profits by withholding information about the company's costs. But he challenged that impulse – he saw that it made more sense in the long run to counteract it. His emotional self-regulation paid off in strong, lasting relationships with distributors that benefited the company more than any short-term financial gains would have.

The signs of emotional self-regulation, therefore, are easy to see: a propensity for reflection

10

and thoughtfulness; comfort with ambiguity and change; and integrity – an ability to say no to impulsive urges. Like self-awareness, self-regulation often does not get its due. People who can master their emotions are sometimes seen as cold fish – their considered responses are taken as a lack of passion. People with fiery temperaments are frequently thought of as "classic" leaders – their outbursts are considered hallmarks of charisma and power. But when such people make it to the top, their impulsiveness often works against them. In my research, extreme displays of negative emotion have never emerged as a driver of good leadership.

If there is one trait that virtually all effective leaders have, it is motivation – a variety of self-management whereby we mobilize our positive emotions to drive us toward our goals. Motivated leaders are driven to achieve beyond expectations – their own and everyone else's. The key word here is *achieve*. Plenty of people are motivated by external factors, such as a big salary or the status that comes from having an impressive title or being part of a prestigious company. By contrast, those with leadership potential are motivated by a deeply embedded desire to achieve for the sake of achievement. If you are looking for leaders, how can you identify people who are motivated by the drive to achieve rather than by external rewards? The first sign is a passion for the work itself – such people seek out creative challenges, love to learn, and take great pride in a job well done. They also display an unflagging energy to do things better. People with such energy often seem restless with the status quo. They are persistent with their questions about why things are done one way rather than another; they are eager to explore new approaches to their work.

A cosmetics company manager, for example, was frustrated that he had to wait two weeks to get sales results from people in the field. He finally tracked down an automated phone system that would beep each of his salespeople at 5 pm every day. An automated message then prompted them to punch in their number to show how many calls and sales they had made that day. The system shortened the feedback time on sales results from weeks to hours. That story illustrates two other common traits of people who are driven to achieve: they are forever raising the performance bar, and they like to keep score.

Take the performance bar first. During performance reviews, people with high levels of motivation might ask to be "stretched" by their superiors. Of course, an employee who combines self-awareness with internal motivation will recognize her limits, but she won't settle for objectives that seem too easy to fulfill. And it follows naturally that people who are driven to do better also want a way of tracking progress – their own, their team's, and their company's. Whereas people with low achievement motivation are often fuzzy about results, those with high achievement motivation often keep score by tracking such hard measures as profitability or market share. Interestingly, people with high motivation remain optimistic even when the score is against them. In such cases, self-regulation combines with achievement motivation to overcome the frustration and depression that come after a setback or failure.

EMPATHY

Of all the dimensions of emotional intelligence, empathy is the most easily recognized. We have all felt the empathy of a sensitive teacher or friend; we have all been struck by its absence in an unfeeling coach or boss. But when it comes to business, we rarely hear people praised, let alone rewarded, for their empathy. The very word seems unbusinesslike, out of place amid the tough realities of the marketplace. But empathy doesn't mean a kind of "I'm OK, you're OK" mushiness. For a leader, it doesn't mean adopting other people's emotions as one's own and trying to please everybody. That would be a nightmare – it would make action impossible. Rather, empathy means thoughtfully considering employees' feelings – along with other factors – in the process of making intelligent decisions. For an example of empathy in action, consider what happened when two giant brokerage companies merged, creating redundant jobs in all their divisions. One division manager called his people together and gave a gloomy speech that emphasized the number of people who would soon be fired. The manager of another division gave his people a different kind of speech. He was up-front about his own worry and confusion, and he promised to keep people informed and to treat everyone fairly. The difference between these two managers was empathy. The first manager was too worried about his own fate to consider the feelings of his anxiety-stricken colleagues. The second knew intuitively what his people were feeling, and he acknowledged their fears with his words. Is it any surprise that the first manager saw his division sink as many demoralized people, especially the most talented, departed? By contrast, the second manager continued to be a strong leader, his best people stayed, and his division remained as productive as ever.

Empathy is particularly important today as a component of leadership for at least three reasons: the increasing use of teams, the rapid pace of globalization; and the growing need to retain talent. Consider the challenge of leading a team. As anyone who has ever been a part of one can attest, teams are cauldrons of bubbling emotions. They are often charged with reaching a consensus – which is hard enough with two people and much more difficult as the numbers increase. Even in groups with as few as four or five members, alliances form and clashing agendas get set. A team's leader must be able to sense and understand the viewpoints of everyone around the table. That's exactly what a marketing manager at a large information technology company was able to do when she was appointed to lead a troubled team. The group was in turmoil, overloaded by work and missing deadlines. Tensions were high among the members. Tinkering with procedures was not enough to bring the group together and make it an effective part of the company. So the manager took several steps. In a series of one-on-one sessions, she took the time to listen to everyone in the group – what was frustrating them, how they rated their colleagues, whether they felt they had been ignored. And then she directed the team in a way that brought it together: She encouraged people to speak more openly about their frustrations, and she helped people raise constructive complaints during meetings. In short, her empathy allowed her to understand her team's emotional makeup. The result was not just heightened collaboration among members but also added business, as the team was called on for help by a wider range of internal clients.

Globalization is another reason for the rising importance of empathy for business leaders. Cross-cultural dialogue can easily lead to miscues and misunderstandings. Empathy is an antidote. People who have it are attuned to subtleties in body language; they can hear the message beneath the words being spoken. Beyond that, they have a deep understanding of both the existence and the importance of cultural and ethnic differences. Consider the case of an American consultant whose team had just pitched a project to a potential Japanese client. In its dealings with Americans, the team was accustomed to being bombarded with questions after such a proposal, but this time it was greeted with a long silence. Other members of the team, taking the silence as disapproval, were ready to pack and leave. The lead consultant gestured them to stop. Although he was not particularly familiar with Japanese culture, he read the client's face and posture and sensed not rejection but interest – even deep consideration. He was right: when the client finally spoke, it was to give the consulting firm the job.

Finally, empathy plays a key role in the retention of talent, particularly in today's information economy. Leaders have always needed empathy to develop and keep good people, but today the stakes are higher. When good people leave, they take the company's knowledge with them. That's where coaching and mentoring come in. It has repeatedly been shown that coaching and mentoring pay off not just in better performance but also in increased job satisfaction and decreased turnover. But what makes coaching and mentoring work best is the nature of the relationship. Outstanding coaches and mentors get inside the heads of the people they are helping. They sense how to give effective feedback. They know when to push for better performance and when to hold back. In the way they motivate their protégés they demonstrate empathy in action. In what is probably sounding like a refrain, let me repeat that empathy doesn't get much respect in business. People wonder how leaders can make hard decisions if they are "feeling" for all the people who will be affected. But leaders with empathy do more than sympathize with people around them: They use their knowledge to improve their companies in subtle but important ways.

SOCIAL SKILL

The first two components of emotional intelligence are self-management skills. The last two, empathy and social skill, concern a person's ability to manage relationships with others. As a component of emotional intelligence, social skill is not as simple as it sounds. It's not just a matter of friendliness – although people with high levels of social skill are rarely mean-spirited. Social skill, rather, is friendliness with a purpose: moving people in the direction you desire, whether that's agreement on a new marketing strategy or enthusiasm about a new product.

Socially skilled people tend to have a wide circle of acquaintances, and they have a knack for finding common ground with people of all kinds – a knack for building rapport. That doesn't mean they socialize continually; it means they work according to the assumption that nothing important gets done alone. Such people have a network in place when the time for action comes. Social skill is the culmination of the other dimensions of emotional intelligence. People tend to be very effective at managing relationships when they can understand and control their own emotions and can empathize with the feelings of others.

Even motivation contributes to social skill. Remember that people who are driven to achieve tend to be optimistic, even in the face of setbacks or failure. When people are upbeat, their "glow" is cast upon conversations and other social encounters. They are popular, and for good reason. Because it is the outcome of the other dimensions of emotional intelligence, social skill is recognizable on the job in many ways that will by now sound familiar. Socially skilled people, for instance, are adept at managing teams – that's their empathy at work. Likewise, they are expert persuaders – a manifestation of self-awareness, self-regulation, and empathy combined. Given those skills, good persuaders know when to make an emotional plea, for instance, and when an appeal to reason will work better. And motivation, when publicly visible, makes such people excellent collaborators; their passion for the work spreads to others, and they are driven to find solutions.

But sometimes social skill shows itself in ways the other emotional intelligence components do not. For instance, socially skilled people may at times appear not to be working while at work. They seem to be idly schmoozing – chatting in the hallways with colleagues or joking around with people who are not even connected to their "real" jobs. Socially skilled people, however, don't think it makes sense to arbitrarily limit the scope of their relationships. They build bonds widely because they know that in these fluid times, they may need help someday from people they are just getting to know today.

For example, consider the case of an executive in the strategy department of a global computer manufacturer. By 1993, he was convinced that the company's future lay with the Internet. Over the course of the next year, he found kindred spirits and used his social skill to stitch together a virtual community that cut across levels, divisions, and nations. He then used this de facto team to put up a corporate Web site, among the first by a major company. And, on his own initiative, with no budget or formal status, he signed up the company to participate in an annual Internet industry convention. Calling on his allies and persuading various divisions to donate funds, he recruited more than 50 people from a dozen different units to represent the company at the convention. Management took notice: within a year of the conference, the executive's team formed the basis for the company's first Internet division, and he was formally put in charge of it. To get there, the executive had ignored conventional boundaries, forging and maintaining connections with people in every corner of the organization.

Is social skill considered a key leadership capability in most companies? The answer is yes, especially when compared with the other components of emotional intelligence. People seem to know intuitively that leaders need to manage relationships effectively; no leader is an island. After all, the leader's task is to get work done through other people, and social skill makes that possible. A leader who cannot express her empathy may as well not have it at all. And a leader's motivation will be useless if he cannot communicate his passion to the organization. Social skill allows leaders to put their emotional intelligence to work.

It would be foolish to assert that good old-fashioned IQ and technical ability are not important ingredients in strong leadership. But the recipe would not be complete without emotional intelligence. It was once thought that the components of emotional intelligence were "nice to have" in business leaders. But now we know that, for the sake of performance, these are ingredients that leaders "need to have." It is fortunate, then, that emotional intelligence can be learned. The process is not easy. It takes time and, most of all, commitment. But the benefits that come from having a well-developed emotional intelligence, both for the individual and for the organization, make it worth the effort.

POSTSCRIPT

Originally Published on LinkedIn.com

EI SKILLS THAT EMPLOYERS WANT NOW

July 07, 2013

Someone recently asked me, "Is emotional intelligence as important in today's job market compared to 1995?", when I wrote my first book on the topic.

More important than ever, I'd say. Here's why. For one, the global job market is demanding more of prospective employees. And the world's best employers are not just pickier – they are seeking top graduates who also have emotional intelligence strengths.

Of course high performance in academics and the right technical skills still matter. But in today's job market the best employers are looking for something in addition. According to Paul Wiseman, economics writer at the Associated Press, the companies also "want graduates with soft skills." The main ones are:

- **Working well on a team**. As one executive once told a McKinsey consultant, "I have never fired an engineer for bad engineering, but I have fired an engineer for lack of teamwork."

- **Clear, effective communications**. This requires strong cognitive empathy, the ability to understand how the other person thinks. Of course, good listening skills are also important.
- **Adapting well to change**. Such flexibility signifies good self-management.
- **Smooth interactions with a wide variety of people**. This includes customers, clients and workmates from groups different than one's own, and from other cultures.
- **Thinking clearly and solving problems under pressure**. A combination of self-awareness, focus, and quick stress recovery puts the brain in an optimal state for whatever cognitive abilities are needed.

Professional schools are listening. Yale's management school recently announced it will add a test of emotional intelligence to its admissions process.

But emotional intelligence skills can be learned. I prefer the approach of my colleague Richard Boyatzis at Case Western University's Weatherhead School of Management. He teaches his MBA students how to enhance their emotional intelligence competencies. Once they've learned how, they continue to build them throughout their career.

HOW TO EVALUATE YOUR EI

June 27, 2013

'What you need now is emotional intelligence,' was what China's new president told a graduating class last month at their top tech school.

Now Bloomberg's Businessweek tells us that Yale's school of management has added a test of emotional intelligence to its admissions requirements. And how's your emotional intelligence?

Just as for IQ, there are several theoretical models of emotional intelligence, each supported by its own set of research findings. The one I've proposed – which has fared well in predicting actual business performance – looks at a spectrum of EI-based leadership competencies that each helps a leader be more effective.

Here are some questions that will help you reflect on your own mix of strengths and limits in EI. This is not a "test" of EI, but a "taste" to get you thinking about your own competencies:

- Are you usually aware of your feelings and why you feel that way?

- Are you aware of your limitations, as well as your personal strengths, as a leader?

- Can you manage your distressing emotions well – e.g., recover quickly when you get upset or stressed?

- Can you adapt smoothly to changing realities?

- Do you keep your focus on your main goals, and know the steps it takes to get there?

- Can you usually sense the feelings of the people you interact with and understand their way of seeing things?

- Do you have a knack for persuasion and using your influence effectively?

- Can you guide a negotiation to a satisfactory agreement, and help settle conflicts?

- Do you work well on a team, or prefer to work on your own?

And the good news: emotional intelligence competencies can be upgraded.

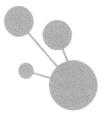

LEADERSHIP THAT
GETS RESULTS

Originally published in the Harvard Business
Review, March 2000

Ask any group of businesspeople the
question "What do effective leaders do?" and
you'll hear a sweep of answers: leaders set strategy;
they motivate; they create a mission; they build a
culture.

Then ask "What should leaders do?" If the
group is seasoned, you'll likely hear one response:
the leader's singular job is to get results.

But how? The mystery of what leaders can
and ought to do in order to spark the best performance
from their people is age-old. Still, effective leadership
eludes many people and organizations. One reason
is that until recently, virtually no quantitative
research has demonstrated which precise leadership
behaviors yield positive results.

Leadership experts proffer advice based on
inference, experience, and instinct. Sometimes that
advice is right on target; sometimes it's not.

Research by the consulting firm Hay/
McBer, which draws on a random sample of 3,871
executives selected from a database of more than
20,000 executives worldwide, takes much of the

mystery out of effective leadership. The research found six distinct leadership styles, each springing from different components of emotional intelligence. The styles, taken individually, appear to have a direct and unique impact on the working atmosphere of a company, division, or team, and in turn, on its financial performance. And perhaps most important, the research indicates that leaders with the best results do not rely on only one leadership style; they use many or most of them in a given week – seamlessly and in different measure – depending on the business situation.

Imagine the styles, then, as the array of clubs in a golf pro's bag. Over the course of a game, the pro picks and chooses clubs based on the demands of the shot. Sometimes he has to ponder his selection, but usually it is automatic. The pro senses the challenge ahead, swiftly pulls out the right tool, and elegantly puts it to work. That's how high-impact leaders operate, too.

What are the six styles of leadership? Each style, by name and brief description alone, will likely resonate with anyone who leads, is led, or as is the case with most of us, does both. Authoritative leaders mobilize people toward a vision. Affiliative leaders create emotional bonds and harmony. Democratic leaders build consensus through participation. Pacesetting leaders expect excellence and self-direction. Coaching leaders develop people for the future. And coercive leaders demand immediate compliance.

Close your eyes and you can surely imagine a colleague who uses any one of these styles. You most likely use at least one yourself. What is new in this research, then, is its implications for action. First, it offers a fine-grained understanding of how different leadership styles affect performance and results. Second, it offers clear guidance on when a manager should switch between them. It also strongly suggests that switching flexibly is well advised. New, too, is the research's finding that each leadership style springs from different components of emotional intelligence.

MEASURING LEADERSHIP'S IMPACT

The late David McClelland, a noted Harvard University psychologist found that leaders with strengths in a critical mass of six or more emotional intelligence competencies were far more effective than peers who lacked such strengths. For instance, when he analyzed the performance of division heads at a global food and beverage company, he found that among leaders with this critical mass of competence, 87 percent placed in the top third for annual salary bonuses based on their business performance. More telling, their divisions outperformed yearly revenue targets by 15 to 20 percent on average.

Those executives who lacked emotional intelligence were rarely rated as outstanding in their annual performance reviews, and their divisions underperformed by an average of almost 20 percent. The research on leadership styles set out to gain a more molecular view of the links between leadership and emotional intelligence, and climate and performance. A team of McClelland's colleagues, headed by Mary Fontaine and Ruth Jacobs from what is now the McClelland Institute at the Boston office of HayGroup, studied data about or observed thousands of executives, noting specific behaviors and their impact on climate.

How did each individual motivate direct reports? Manage change initiatives? Handle crises? It was a later phase of the research that identified how emotional intelligence capabilities drive the six leadership styles. How does he rate in terms of self-control and social skill? Does a leader show high or low levels of empathy? The team tested each executive's immediate sphere of influence for its climate.

"Climate" is not an amorphous term. First defined by psychologists George Litwin and Richard Stringer and later refined by McClelland and his colleagues, it refers to six key factors that influence an organization's working environment: its flexibility – that is, how free employees feel to innovate unencumbered by red tape; their sense of responsibility to the organization; the level of standards that people set; the sense of accuracy about performance feedback and aptness of rewards; the clarity people have about mission and values; and finally, the level of commitment to a common purpose. All six leadership styles have a measurable effect on each aspect of climate.

Further, when the team looked at the impact of climate on financial results – such as return on sales, revenue growth, efficiency, and profitability – they found a direct correlation between the two. Leaders who used styles that positively affected the climate had decidedly better financial results than those who did not. That is not to say that organizational climate is the only driver of performance. Economic conditions and competitive dynamics matter enormously. But this analysis strongly suggests that climate accounts for nearly a third of results. And that's simply too much of an impact to ignore.

Executives use six main leadership styles, but only four of the six consistently have a positive effect on climate and results. Let's look then at each style of leadership in detail, starting with the Authoritative (or Visionary) Style.

THE AUTHORITATIVE STYLE

Tom was the vice-president of marketing at a floundering national restaurant chain that specialized in pizza. Needless to say, the company's poor performance troubled the senior managers, but they were at a loss for what to do. Every Monday, they met to review recent sales, struggling to come up with fixes. To Tom, the approach didn't make sense. "We were always trying to figure out why our sales were down last week. We had the whole company looking backward instead of figuring out what we had to do tomorrow."

Tom saw an opportunity to change people's way of thinking at an off-site strategy meeting. There, the conversation began with stale truisms: the company had to drive up shareholder wealth and increase return on assets. Tom believed those concepts didn't have the power to inspire a restaurant manager to be innovative or to do better than a good-enough job.

So Tom made a bold move. In the middle of a meeting, he made an impassioned plea for his colleagues to think from the customer's perspective. Customers want convenience, he said. The company was not in the restaurant business, it was in the business of distributing high quality, convenient-to-get pizza. That notion and nothing else should drive everything the company did.

With his vibrant enthusiasm and clear vision – the hallmarks of the authoritative style – Tom filled a leadership vacuum at the company. Indeed, his concept became the core of the new mission statement. But this conceptual breakthrough was just the beginning. Tom made sure that the mission statement was built into the company's strategic planning process as the designated driver of growth. And he ensured that the vision was articulated so that local restaurant managers understood they were the key to the company's success and were free to find new ways to distribute pizza.

Changes came quickly. Within weeks, many local managers started guaranteeing fast new delivery times. Even better, they started to act like entrepreneurs, finding ingenious locations to open new branches: kiosks on busy street corners and in bus and train stations, even from carts in airports and hotel lobbies.

Tom's success was no fluke. The research indicates that of the six leadership styles, the authoritative one is most effective, driving up every aspect of climate. Take clarity. The authoritative leader is a visionary; he motivates people by making clear to them how their work fits into a larger vision for the organization. People who work for such leaders understand that what they do matters and why.

Authoritative leadership also maximizes commitment to the organization's goals and strategy. By framing the individual tasks within a grand vision, the authoritative leader defines standards that revolve around that vision. When he gives performance feedback – whether positive or negative – the singular criterion is whether or not that performance furthers the vision. The standards for success are clear to all, as are the rewards.

Finally, consider the style's impact on flexibility. An authoritative leader states the end but generally gives people plenty of leeway to devise their own means. Authoritative leaders give people the freedom to innovate, experiment, and take calculated risks. Because of its positive impact, the authoritative style works well in almost any business situation. But it is particularly effective when a business is adrift. An authoritative leader charts a new course and sells his people on a fresh long-term vision.

The authoritative style, powerful though it may be, will not work in every situation. The approach fails, for instance, when a leader is working with a team of experts or peers who are more experienced than he is; they may see the leader as pompous or out-of-touch. Another limitation: if a manager trying to be authoritative becomes overbearing, he can undermine the egalitarian spirit of an effective team. Yet even with such caveats, leaders would be wise to grab for the authoritative "club" more often than not. It may not guarantee a hole in one, but it certainly helps with the long drive.

THE COACHING STYLE

A product unit at a global computer company had seen sales plummet from twice as much as its competitors to only half as much. So Lawrence, the president of the manufacturing division, decided to close the unit and reassign its people and products. Upon hearing the news, James, the head of the doomed unit, decided to go over his boss's head and plead his case to the CEO.

What did Lawrence do? Instead of blowing up at James, he sat down with his rebellious direct report and talked over not just the decision to close the division but also James's future. He explained to James how moving to another division would help him develop new skills. It would make him a better leader and teach him more about the company's business. Lawrence acted more like a counselor than a traditional boss.

He listened to James's concerns and hopes, and he shared his own. He said he believed James had grown stale in his current job; it was, after all, the only place he'd worked in the company. He predicted that James would blossom in a new role. The conversation then took a practical turn. James had not yet had his meeting with the CEO – the one he had impetuously demanded when he heard of his division's closing. Knowing this – and also knowing that the CEO unwaveringly supported the closing – Lawrence took the time to coach James on how to present his case in that meeting. "You don't get an audience with the CEO very often," he noted, "let's make sure you impress him with your thoughtfulness."

He advised James not to plead his personal case but to focus on the business unit: "If he thinks you're in there for your own glory, he'll throw you out faster than you walked through the door." And he urged him to put his ideas in writing; the CEO always appreciated that.

Lawrence's reason for coaching instead of scolding? "James is a good guy, very talented and promising," the executive explained to us, "and I don't want this to derail his career. I want him to stay with the company, I want him to work out, I want him to learn, I want him to benefit and grow. Just because he screwed up doesn't mean he's terrible."

Lawrence's actions illustrate the coaching style par excellence. Coaching leaders help employees identify their unique strengths and weaknesses and tie them to their personal and career aspirations. They encourage employees to establish long-term development goals and help them conceptualize a plan for attaining them. They make agreements with their employees about their role and responsibilities in enacting development plans, and they give plentiful instruction and feedback.

Coaching leaders excel at delegating; they give employees challenging assignments, even if that means the tasks won't be accomplished quickly. In other words, these leaders are willing to put up with short-term failure if it furthers long-term learning.

Of the six styles, our research found that the coaching style is used least often. Many leaders told us they don't have the time in this high-pressure economy for the slow and tedious work of teaching people and helping them grow. But after a first session, it takes little or no extra time. Leaders who ignore this style are passing up a powerful tool; its impact on climate and performance are markedly positive.

Admittedly, there is a paradox in coaching's positive effect on business performance because coaching focuses primarily on personal development, not on immediate work-related tasks. Even so, coaching improves results. The reason: it requires constant dialogue, and that dialogue has a way of pushing up every driver of climate. Take flexibility, for example. When an employee knows his boss watches him and cares about what he does, he feels free to experiment. After all, he's sure to get quick and constructive feedback.

Similarly, the ongoing dialogue of coaching guarantees that people know what is expected of them and how their work fits into a larger vision or strategy. That affects responsibility and clarity. Coaching helps with commitment, too, because the style's implicit message is, "I believe in you, I'm investing in you, and I expect your best efforts." Employees very often rise to that challenge with their hearts, minds, and souls.

The coaching style works well in many business situations, but it is perhaps most effective when people on the receiving end are "up for it." For instance, the coaching style works particularly well when employees are already aware of their weaknesses and would like to improve their performance. Similarly, the style works well when employees realize how cultivating new abilities can help them advance. In short, it works best with employees who want to be coached.

By contrast, the coaching style makes little sense when employees, for whatever reason, are resistant to learning or changing their ways. And it flops if the leader lacks the expertise to help the employee along. The fact is, many managers are unfamiliar with or simply inept at coaching, particularly when it comes to giving ongoing performance feedback that motivates rather than creates fear or apathy.

Some companies have realized the positive impact of the style and are trying to make it a core competence. At some companies, a significant portion of annual bonuses are tied to an executive's development of his or her direct reports. But many organizations have yet to take full advantage of this leadership style. Although the coaching style may not scream "bottom-line results," it delivers them.

THE AFFILIATIVE STYLE

If the authoritative leader urges, "Come with me," the affiliative leader says, "People come first." This leadership style revolves around people – its proponents value individuals and their emotions more than tasks and goals. The affiliative leader strives to keep employees happy and to create harmony among them. He manages by building strong emotional bonds and then reaping the benefit of such an approach; namely, fierce loyalty.

The style also has a markedly positive effect on communication. People who like one another a lot talk a lot. They share ideas; they share inspiration. And the style drives up flexibility; friends trust one another, allowing habitual innovation and risk taking. Flexibility also rises because the affiliative leader, like a parent who adjusts household rules for a maturing adolescent, doesn't impose unnecessary strictures on how employees get their work done. They give people the freedom to do their job in the way they think is most effective.

The affiliative leader offers ample positive feedback, providing a sense of recognition and reward for work well done. Such feedback has special potency in the workplace because it is all too rare: outside of an annual review, most people usually get no feedback on their day-to-day efforts – or only negative feedback. That makes the affiliative leader's positive words all the more motivating.

Finally, affiliative leaders are masters at building a sense of belonging. They are, for instance, likely to take their direct reports out for a meal or a drink, one-on-one, to see how they're doing. They will bring in a cake to celebrate a group accomplishment. They are natural relationship builders.

Joe Torre, at one time the heart and soul of the New York Yankees, was a classic affiliative leader. During the 1999 World Series, Torre tended ably to the psyches of his players as they endured the emotional pressure cooker of a pennant race. All season long, he made a special point to praise Scott Brosius, whose father had died during the season, for staying committed even as he mourned.

At the celebration party after the team's final game, Torre specifically sought out right fielder Paul O'Neill. Although he had received the news of his father's death that morning, O'Neill chose to play in the decisive game – and he burst into tears the moment it ended. Torre made a point of acknowledging O'Neill's personal struggle, calling him a "warrior." Torre also used the spotlight of the victory celebration to praise two players whose return the following year was threatened by contract disputes. In doing so, he sent a clear message to the team and to the club's owner that he valued the players immensely – too much to lose them.

Along with ministering to the emotions of his people, an affiliative leader may also tend to his own emotions openly. The year his brother was near death awaiting a heart transplant, Torre shared his worries with his players. He also spoke candidly with the team about his treatment for prostate cancer. The affiliative style's generally positive impact makes it a good all-weather approach, but leaders should employ it particularly when trying to build team harmony, increase morale, improve communication, or repair broken trust.

For instance, one executive was hired to replace a ruthless team leader. The former leader had taken credit for his employees' work and had attempted to pit them against one another. His efforts ultimately failed, but the team he left behind was suspicious and weary. The new executive managed to mend the situation by unstintingly showing emotional honesty and rebuilding ties. Several months in, her leadership had created a renewed sense of commitment and energy.

Despite its benefits, the affiliative style should not be used alone. Its exclusive focus on praise can allow poor performance to go uncorrected; employees may perceive that mediocrity is tolerated. And because affiliative leaders rarely offer constructive advice on how to improve, employees must figure out how to do so on their own. When people need clear directives to navigate through complex challenges, the affiliative style leaves them rudderless.

Indeed, if overly relied on, this style can actually steer a group to failure. Perhaps that is why many affiliative leaders, including Torre, use this style in close conjunction with the authoritative style. Authoritative leaders state a vision, set standards, and let people know how their work is furthering the group's goals. Alternate that with the caring, nurturing approach of the affiliative leader, and you have a potent combination.

THE DEMOCRATIC STYLE

Sister Mary ran a Catholic school system in a large metropolitan area. One of the schools – the only private school in an impoverished neighborhood – had been losing money for years, and the archdiocese could no longer afford to keep it open. When Sister Mary eventually got the order to shut it down, she didn't just lock the doors.

She called a meeting of all the teachers and staff at the school and explained to them the details of the financial crisis – the first time anyone working at the school had been included in the business side of the institution. She asked for their ideas on ways to keep the school open and on how to handle the closing, should it come to that. Sister Mary spent much of her time at the meeting just listening. She did the same at later meetings for school parents and for the community and during a successive series of meetings for the school's teachers and staff.

After two months of meetings, the consensus was clear: the school would have to close. A plan was made to transfer students to other schools in the Catholic system. The final outcome was no different than if Sister Mary had gone ahead and closed the school the day she was told to. But by allowing the school's constituents to reach that decision collectively, Sister Mary received none of the backlash that would have accompanied such a move. People mourned the loss of the school, but they understood its inevitability. Virtually no one objected.

Compare that with the experiences of a priest in our research who headed another Catholic school. He, too, was told to shut it down. And he did – by fiat. The result was disastrous: parents filed lawsuits, teachers and parents picketed, and local newspapers ran editorials attacking his decision. It took a year to resolve the disputes before he could finally go ahead and close the school.

Sister Mary exemplifies the democratic style and its benefits in action. By spending time getting people's ideas and buy-in, a leader builds trust, respect, and commitment. By letting workers themselves have a say in decisions that affect their goals and how they do their work, the democratic leader drives up flexibility and responsibility. And by listening to employees' concerns, the democratic leader learns what to do to keep morale high. Finally, because they have a say in setting their goals and the standards for evaluating success, people operating in a democratic system tend to be very realistic about what can and cannot be accomplished.

However, the democratic style has its drawbacks, which is why its impact on climate is not as high as some of the other styles. One of its more exasperating consequences can be endless meetings where ideas are mulled over, consensus remains elusive, and the only visible result is scheduling more meetings. Some democratic leaders use the style to put off making crucial decisions, hoping that enough thrashing things out will eventually yield a blinding insight. In reality, their people end up feeling confused and leaderless. Such an approach can even escalate conflicts.

When does the style work best? This approach is ideal when a leader is himself uncertain about the best direction to take and needs ideas and guidance from able employees. And even if a leader has a strong vision, the democratic style works well to generate fresh ideas for executing that vision. The democratic style, of course, makes much less sense when employees are not competent or informed enough to offer sound advice. And it almost goes without saying that building consensus is wrongheaded in times of crisis.

Take the case of a CEO whose computer company was severely threatened by changes in the market. He always sought consensus about what to do. As competitors stole customers and customers' needs changed, he kept appointing committees to consider the situation. When the market made a sudden shift because of a new technology, the CEO froze in his tracks.

The board replaced him before he could appoint yet another task force to consider the situation. The new CEO, while occasionally democratic and affiliative, relied heavily on the authoritative style, especially in his first months.

THE PACESETTING STYLE

The pacesetting style has its place in the leader's repertory, but it should be used sparingly. That's not what we expected to find. After all, the hallmarks of the pacesetting style sound admirable. The leader sets extremely high performance standards and exemplifies them himself. He is obsessive about doing things better and faster, and he asks the same of everyone around him. He quickly pinpoints poor performers and demands more from them. If they don't rise to the occasion, he replaces them with people who can.

You would think such an approach would improve results, but it doesn't. In fact, the pacesetting style destroys climate. Many employees feel overwhelmed by the pacesetter's demands for excellence, and their morale drops. Guidelines for working may be clear in the leader's head, but she does not state them clearly; she expects people to know what to do and even thinks, "If I have to tell you, you're the wrong person for the job."

Work becomes not a matter of doing one's best along a clear course so much as second-guessing what the leader wants. At the same time, people often feel that the pacesetter doesn't trust them to work in their own way or to take initiative. Flexibility and responsibility evaporate; work becomes so task-focused and routinized it's boring. As for rewards, the pacesetter either gives no feedback on how people are doing or jumps in to take over when he thinks they're lagging. And if the leader should leave, people feel directionless – they're so used to "the expert" setting the rules. Finally, commitment dwindles under the regime of a pacesetting leader because people have no sense of how their personal efforts fit into the big picture.

For an example of the pacesetting style, take the case of Sam, a biochemist in R&D at a large pharmaceutical company. Sam's superb technical expertise made him an early star: he was the one everyone turned to when they needed help. Soon he was promoted to head of a team developing a new product. The other scientists on the team were as competent and self-motivated as Sam; his métier as team leader became offering himself as a model of how to do first-class scientific work under tremendous deadline pressure, pitching in when needed. His team completed its task in record time.

But then came a new assignment: Sam was put in charge of R&D for his entire division. As his tasks expanded and he had to articulate a vision, coordinate projects, delegate responsibility, and help develop others, Sam began to slip. Not trusting that his subordinates were as capable as he was, he became a micromanager, obsessed with details and taking over for others when their performance slackened. Instead of trusting them to improve with guidance and development, Sam found himself working nights and weekends after stepping in to take over for the head of a floundering research team. Finally, his own boss suggested, to his relief, that he return to his old job as head of a product development team.

Although Sam faltered, the pacesetting style isn't always a disaster. The approach works well when all employees are self-motivated, highly competent, and need little direction or coordination – for example, it can work for leaders of highly skilled and self-motivated professionals, like R&D groups or legal teams. And, given a talented team to lead, pacesetting does exactly that: gets work done on time or even ahead of schedule. Yet like any leadership style, pacesetting should never be used by itself.

THE COERCIVE STYLE

A computer company was in crisis mode – its sales and profits were falling, its stock was losing value precipitously, and its shareholders were in an uproar. The board brought in a new CEO with a reputation as a turnaround artist. He set to work chopping jobs, selling off divisions, and making the tough decisions that should have been executed years before. The company was saved, at least in the short-term. From the start, though, the CEO created a reign of terror, bullying and demeaning his executives, roaring his displeasure at the slightest misstep. The company's top echelons were decimated not just by his erratic firings but also by defections. The CEO's direct reports, frightened by his tendency to blame the bearer of bad news, stopped bringing him any news at all. Morale was at an all-time low – a fact reflected in another downturn in the business after the short-term recovery. The CEO was eventually fired by the board of directors.

It's easy to understand why of all the leadership styles, the coercive one is the least effective in most situations. Consider what the style does to an organization's climate. Flexibility is the hardest hit. The leader's extreme top-down decision-making kills new ideas on the vine. People feel so disrespected that they think, "I won't even bring my ideas up – they'll only be shot down." Likewise, people's sense of responsibility evaporates: unable to act on their own initiative, they lose their sense of ownership and feel little accountability for their performance. Some become so resentful they adopt the attitude, "I'm not going to help this bastard."

Coercive leadership also has a damaging effect on the rewards system. Most high performing workers are motivated by more than money – they seek the satisfaction of work well done. The coercive style erodes such pride. And finally, the style undermines one of the leader's prime tools – motivating people by showing them how their job fits into a grand, shared mission. Such a loss, measured in terms of diminished clarity and commitment, leaves people alienated from their own jobs, wondering, "How does any of this matter?"

Given the impact of the coercive style, you might assume it should never be applied. The research, however, uncovered a few occasions when it worked masterfully.

Take the case of a division president who was brought in to change the direction of a food company that was losing money. His first act was to have the executive conference room demolished. To him, the room – with its long marble table that looked like "the deck of the Starship Enterprise" –

symbolized the tradition-bound formality that was paralyzing the company. The destruction of the room, and the subsequent move to a smaller, more informal setting, sent a message no one could miss, and the division's culture changed quickly in its wake.

That said, the coercive style should be used only with extreme caution and in the few situations when it is absolutely imperative, such as during a turnaround or when a hostile takeover is looming. In those cases, the coercive style can break failed business habits and shock people into new ways of working. It is always appropriate during a genuine emergency, like in the aftermath of an earthquake or a fire. And it can work with problem employees with whom all else has failed.

But if a leader relies solely on this style or continues to use it once the emergency passes, the long-term impact of his insensitivity to the morale and feelings of those he leads will be ruinous.

LEADERS NEED MANY STYLES

Many studies, including this one, have shown that the more styles a leader exhibits, the better. Leaders who have mastered four or more – especially the authoritative, democratic, affiliative, and coaching styles – have the very best climate and business performance. And the most effective leaders switch flexibly among the leadership styles as needed. Although that may sound daunting, we've witnessed it more often than you might guess, at both large corporations and tiny start-ups, by seasoned veterans who could explain exactly how and why they lead and by entrepreneurs who claim to lead by gut alone.

Such leaders don't mechanically match their style to fit a checklist of situations – they are far more fluid. They are exquisitely sensitive to the impact they are having on others and seamlessly adjust their style to get the best results. These are leaders, for example, who can read in the first minutes of conversation that a talented but underperforming employee has been demoralized by an unsympathetic, do-it-the-way-I-tell-you manager and needs to be inspired through a reminder of why her work matters. Or that leader might choose to reenergize the employee by asking her about her dreams and aspirations and finding ways to make her job more challenging. Or that initial conversation might signal that the employee needs an ultimatum: improve or leave.

For an example of fluid leadership in action, consider Joan, the general manager of a major division at a global food and beverage company. Joan was appointed to her job while the division was in a deep crisis. It had not made its profit targets for six years; in the most recent year, it had missed by $50 million. Morale among the top management team was miserable; mistrust and resentments were rampant.

Joan's directive from above was clear: turn the division around. Joan did so with a nimbleness in switching among leadership styles that is rare. From the start, she realized she had a short window to demonstrate effective leadership and to establish rapport and trust. She also knew that she urgently needed to be informed about what was not working, so her first task was to listen to key people.

During her first week on the job she had lunch and dinner meetings with each member of the management team. Joan sought to get each person's understanding of the current situation. But her focus was not so much on learning how each person diagnosed the problem as on getting to know each manager as a person. Here Joan employed the affiliative style: she explored their lives, dreams, and aspirations.

She also stepped into the coaching role, looking for ways she could help the team members achieve what they wanted in their careers. For instance, one manager who had been getting feedback that he was a poor team player confided his worries to her. He thought he was a good team member, but he was plagued by persistent complaints. Recognizing that he was a talented executive and a valuable asset to the company, Joan made an agreement with him to point out (in private) when his actions undermined his goal of being seen as a team player.

She followed the one-on-one conversations with a three-day off-site meeting. Her goal here was team building, so that everyone would own whatever solution for the business problems emerged. Her initial stance at the offsite meeting was that of a democratic leader; she encouraged everyone to express freely their frustrations and complaints.

The next day, Joan had the group focus on solutions: each person made three specific proposals about what needed to be done. As Joan clustered the suggestions, a natural consensus emerged about priorities for the business, such as cutting costs. As the group came up with specific action plans, Joan got the commitment and buy-in she sought.

With that vision in place, Joan shifted into the authoritative style, assigning accountability for each follow-up step to specific executives and holding them responsible for their accomplishment. For example, the division had been dropping prices on products without increasing its volume. One obvious solution was to raise prices, but the previous VP of sales had dithered and had let the problem fester. The new VP of sales now had responsibility to adjust the price points to fix the problem.

Over the following months, Joan's main stance was authoritative. She continually articulated the group's new vision in a way that reminded each member of how his or her role was crucial to achieving these goals. And, especially during the first few weeks of the plan's implementation, Joan felt that the urgency of the business crisis justified an occasional shift into the coercive style should someone fail to meet his or her responsibility. As she put it, "I had to be brutal about this follow-up and make sure this stuff happened. It was going to take discipline and focus."

The results? Every aspect of climate improved. People were innovating. They were talking about the division's vision and crowing about their commitment to new, clear goals. The ultimate proof of Joan's fluid leadership style is written in black ink: after only seven months, her division exceeded its yearly profit target by $5 million.

EXPANDING YOUR REPERTORY

Few leaders, of course, have all six styles in their repertory, and even fewer know when and how to use them. In fact, as these findings have been shown to leaders in many organizations, the most common responses have been, "But I have only two of those!" and, "I can't use all those styles. It wouldn't be natural."

Such feelings are understandable, and in some cases, the antidote is relatively simple: the leader can build a team with members who employ styles she lacks. Take the case of a VP for manufacturing. She successfully ran a global factory system largely by using the affiliative style. She was on the road constantly, meeting with plant managers, attending to their pressing concerns, and letting them know how much she cared about them personally.

She left the division's strategy – extreme efficiency – to a trusted lieutenant with a keen understanding of technology, and she delegated its performance standards to a colleague who was adept at the authoritative approach. She also had a pacesetter on her team who always visited the plants with her.

An alternative approach, and one I would recommend more, is for leaders to expand their own style repertories. To do so, leaders must first understand which emotional intelligence competencies underlie the leadership styles they are lacking. They can then work assiduously to increase their quotient of them.

For instance, an affiliative leader has strengths in three emotional intelligence competencies: in empathy, in building relationships, and in communication. Empathy – sensing how people are feeling in the moment – allows the affiliative leader to respond to employees in a way that is highly congruent with that person's emotions, thus building rapport. The affiliative leader also displays a natural ease in forming new relationships, getting to know someone as a person, and cultivating a bond.

Finally, the outstanding affiliative leader has mastered the art of interpersonal communication, particularly in saying just the right thing or making the apt symbolic gesture at just the right moment. So if you are primarily a pacesetting leader who wants to be able to use the affiliative style more often, you would need to improve your level of empathy and, perhaps, your skills at building relationships or communicating effectively.

As another example, an authoritative leader who wants to add the democratic style to his repertory might need to work on the capabilities of collaboration and communication.

Hour to hour, day to day, week to week, executives must play their leadership styles like golf clubs, the right one at just the right time and in the right measure. The payoff is in the results.

LEADERSHIP STYLES

Leadership Style	How it Builds Resonance	Impact on Office Climate	When is it Appropriate
Visionary (Authoritative)	Moves people toward shared dreams	most strongly positive	when change requires a new vision, or when a clear direction is needed
Coaching	Connects what a person wants with the team's goals	highly positive	to help a person contribute more effectively to the team
Affiliative	Values people's input and gets commitment through participation	positive	to heal rifts in a team, motivate during successful times or strengthen connections
Democratic	Values people's input and gets commitment through participation	positive	to build buy-in or consensus, or to get valuable input from team members
Pacesetting	sets challenging and exciting goals	often highly negative, because it is poorly executed	to get high quality results from a motivated and competent team
Commanding (Coercive)	soothes fears by giving clear direction in an emergency	often highly negative, because it is misused	in crisis, to kick start a turnaround

POSTSCRIPT

Originally Published on LinkedIn.com

CONNECT WITH THOSE YOU LEAD

May 12, 2013

You've got your urgent to-do list in mind, and someone comes up to you and wants to chat. It can be an irritating interruption – or a chance to switch gears for a moment, really connect, and then move on.

Which way you go can have major implications for how you lead. If you always see the other person as a bother, and never stop to connect, that may be a clue you are caught in a counter-productive mode. Call it "duty-bound."

Or, say, you're on a tight deadline for a project, and someone you're counting on for part of it makes a less-than-perfect contribution. That's disappointing, for sure. But how do you react? Do you think about what it would take to help that person get up to speed in the future? Or do you focus in on what was wrong, and dismiss that person as a failure – someone you can no longer count on?

If you only ever do the latter, zeroing

in on people's flaws rather than their potential, you're acting like a perfectionist.

These cases came up in a workshop I gave with my wife, Tara Bennett-Goleman. Those leadership examples were offered up by a coach – she calls herself an "organizational therapist" – who said, "It really helps to have a name for these patterns. Then you know where to focus in coaching."

The diagnostic labels for these patterns are called "modes" in Tara's book *Mind Whispering*. While we're in the "duty-bound" mode we focus on getting tasks done and ignore the people around us. That can be productive in the short-term, but if you are a leader and you are too rigid in this, you will fail to connect with those you lead. And it is only by connecting that you can guide, inspire, listen, communicate, motivate or influence – in other words, lead.

In the "perfectionist" mode you fixate on people's failings. Perfectionist leaders only give failing grades – they never praise good performance. Research on leadership styles finds perfectionists (sometimes called "pacesetters") have a negative impact on their direct reports' emotional state and performance.

The good news: modes can change. Coaches can help guide this change, and leaders who are highly motivated to improve can do so on their own.

SURVIVING AN S.O.B

June 11, 2013

Having an abusive boss is one of the most stressful situations of any. For one, if it's a supervisor you can't avoid, in addition to the emotional burden of the abuse, there is the added toll of feeling helpless. In the long run this can be a recipe for emotional exhaustion and burnout.

So if you can't change the situation, what can you do? I recommend changing how you react to it. Take control of your internal world.

This reminds me of a time in my own career when I worked at a publication where a new editor – my boss – was particularly hostile to me. I couldn't do anything about him being the boss. But I could do something about my reactions to him.

I had been an off-again, on-again meditator. Now I became a serious one, meditating for 45 minutes each day before heading off to work.

I knew this would help me deal with that toxic boss, from research I had done years before while at Harvard. I had done a physiological study of meditation as an antidote to stress reactivity. I found that meditators, like everyone else, had a jump in heart rate, sweat response and so on in reaction to stress. But they recovered more quickly. This ability to recover quickly from stress arousal is the key to resilience.

For me that made all the difference in being able to get my work done well, even with a bad boss. Instead of my mind being preoccupied by anxiety, I could drop my worries about my boss and keep my focus on the work I had to do. And that helped me survive until he got a promotion – and the whole department celebrated his departure.

PRIMAL LEADERSHIP:

THE HIDDEN DRIVER OF GREAT PERFORMANCE

written with Richard Boyatzis
and Annie McKee

Originally published in the Harvard Business
Review, December 2001

When the theory of emotional intelligence at work began to receive widespread attention, we frequently heard executives say – in the same breath, mind you – "That's incredible," and, "Well, I've known that all along." They were responding to our research that showed an incontrovertible link between an executive's emotional maturity, exemplified by such capabilities as self-awareness and empathy, and his or her financial performance. Simply put, the research showed that "good guys"- that is, emotionally intelligent men and women– finish first.

We've recently compiled two years of new research that we suspect will elicit the same kind of reaction. People will first exclaim, "No way," then quickly add, "But of course." We found that of all the elements affecting bottom-line performance, the importance of the leader's mood and its attendant behaviors are most surprising. That powerful pair set off a chain reaction: The leader's mood and behaviors drive the moods and behaviors of everyone else. A cranky and ruthless boss creates a toxic organization filled with negative underachievers who ignore opportunities; an inspirational, inclusive leader spawns acolytes for whom any challenge is surmountable. The final link in the chain is performance: profit or loss.

Our observation about the overwhelming impact of the leader's "emotional style," as we call it, is not a wholesale departure from our research into emotional intelligence. It does, however, represent a deeper analysis of our earlier assertion that a leader's emotional intelligence creates a certain culture or work environment. High levels of emotional intelligence, our research showed, create climates in which information sharing, trust, healthy risk-taking, and learning flourish. Low levels of emotional intelligence create climates rife with fear and anxiety. Because tense or terrified employees can be very productive in the short term, their organizations may post good results, but they never last.

Our investigation was designed in part to look at how emotional intelligence drives performance – in particular, at how it travels from the leader through the organization to bottom-line results. "What mechanism," we asked, "binds the chain together?" To answer that question, we turned to the latest neurological and psychological research. We also drew on our work with business leaders, observations by our colleagues of hundreds of leaders, and HayGroup data on the leadership styles of thousands of executives. From this body of research, we discovered that emotional intelligence is carried through an organization like electricity through wires. To be more specific, the leader's mood is quite literally contagious, spreading quickly and inexorably throughout the business.

We'll discuss the science of mood contagion in more depth later, but first let's turn to the key implications of our finding. If a leader's mood and accompanying behaviors are indeed such potent drivers of business success, then a leader's premier task – we would even say his primal task – is emotional leadership. A leader needs to make sure that not only is he regularly in an optimistic, authentic, high-energy mood, but also that, through his chosen actions, his followers feel and act that way, too. Managing for financial results, then, begins with the leader managing his inner life so that the right emotional and behavioral chain reaction occurs.

Managing one's inner life is not easy, of course. For many of us, it's our most difficult challenge. And accurately gauging how one's emotions affect others can be just as difficult. We know of one CEO, for example, who was certain that everyone saw him as upbeat and reliable; his direct reports told us they found his cheerfulness strained, even fake, and his decisions erratic. (We call this common disconnect "CEO disease.") The implication is that primal leadership demands more than putting on a game face every day. It requires an executive to determine, through reflective analysis, how his emotional leadership drives the moods and actions of the organization, and then, with equal discipline, to adjust his behavior accordingly.

That's not to say that leaders can't have a bad day or week: Life happens. And our research doesn't suggest that good moods have to be high-pitched or nonstop – optimistic, sincere, and realistic will do. But there is no escaping the conclusion that a leader must first attend to the impact of his mood and behaviors before moving on to his wide panoply of other critical responsibilities. In this article, we introduce a process that executives can follow to assess how others experience their leadership, and we discuss ways to calibrate that impact. But first, we'll look at why moods aren't often discussed in the workplace, how the brain works to make moods contagious, and what you need to know about CEO disease.

NO WAY! YES WAY

When we said earlier that people will likely respond to our new finding by saying "No way," we weren't joking. The fact is, the emotional impact of a leader is almost never discussed in the workplace, let alone in the literature on leadership and performance. For most people, "mood" feels too personal. Even though Americans can be shockingly candid about personal matters, we are also the most legally bound. We can't even ask the age of a job applicant. Thus, a conversation about an executive's mood or the mood he creates in his employees might be construed as an invasion of privacy.

We also might avoid talking about a leader's emotional style and its impact because, frankly, the topic feels soft. When was the last time you evaluated a subordinate's mood as part of her performance appraisal? You may have alluded to it – "Your work is hindered by an often negative perspective," or "Your enthusiasm is terrific" – but it is unlikely you mentioned mood outright, let alone discussed its impact on the organization's results.

And yet our research undoubtedly will elicit a "But of course", reaction, too. Everyone knows how much a leader's emotional state drives performance because everyone has had, at one time or another, the inspirational experience of working for an upbeat manager or the crushing experience of toiling for a sour-spirited boss. The former made everything feel possible, and as a result, stretch goals were achieved, competitors beaten, and new customers won. The latter made work grueling. In the shadow of the boss's dark mood, other parts of the organization became "the enemy," colleagues became suspicious of one another, and customers slipped away.

Our research, and research by other social scientists, confirms the verity of these experiences. There are, of course, rare cases when a brutal boss produces terrific results.

THOSE WICKED BOSSES WHO WIN

Everyone knows of a rude and coercive CEO who, by all appearances, epitomizes the antithesis of emotional intelligence yet seems to reap great business results. If a leader's mood matters so much, how can we explain those mean-spirited, successful SOBs?

First, let's take a closer look at them. Just because a particular executive is the most visible, he may not actually lead the company. A CEO who heads a conglomerate may have no followers to speak of; it's his division heads who actively lead people and affect profitability.

Second, sometimes an SOB leader has strengths that counterbalance his caustic behavior, but they don't attract as much attention in the business press. In his early days at GE, Jack Welch exhibited a strong hand at the helm as he undertook a radical company turnaround. At that time and in that situation, Welch's firm, top-down style was appropriate. What got less press was how Welch subsequently settled into a more emotionally intelligent leadership style, especially when he articulated a new vision for the company and mobilized people to follow it.

Those caveats aside, let's get back to those infamous corporate leaders who seem to have achieved sterling business results despite their brutish approaches to leadership. Skeptics cite Bill Gates, for example, as a leader who gets away with a harsh style that should theoretically damage his company.

But our leadership model, which shows the effectiveness of specific leadership styles in specific situations, puts Gates's supposedly negative behaviors in a different light. Gates is the achievement-driven leader par excellence, in an organization that has cherry-picked highly talented and motivated people. His apparently harsh leadership style – baldly challenging employees to surpass their past performance – can be quite effective when employees are competent, motivated, and need little direction – all characteristics of Microsoft's engineers.

In short, it's all too easy for a skeptic to argue against the importance of leaders who manage their moods by citing a "rough and tough" leader who achieved good business results despite his bad behavior. We contend that there are, of course, exceptions to the rule, and that in some specific business cases an SOB boss resonates just fine. But in general, leaders who are jerks must reform, or else their moods and actions will eventually catch up with them.

The studies are too numerous to mention here, but in aggregate they show that when the leader is in a happy mood, the people around him view everything in a more positive light. That, in turn, makes them optimistic about achieving their goals, enhances their creativity and the efficiency of their decision-making, and predisposes them to be helpful. Research conducted by Alice Isen at Cornell in 1999, for example, found that an upbeat environment fosters mental efficiency, making people better at taking in and understanding information, at using decision rules in complex judgments, and at being flexible in their thinking. Other research directly links mood and financial performance. In 1986, for instance, Martin Seligman and Peter Schulman of the University of Pennsylvania demonstrated that insurance agents who had a "glass half-full" outlook were far more able than their more pessimistic peers to persist despite rejections, and thus, they closed more sales.

Many leaders whose emotional styles create a dysfunctional environment are eventually fired. Of course, that's rarely the stated reason; poor results are. But it doesn't have to end that way. Just as a bad mood can be turned around, so can the spread of toxic feelings from an emotionally inept leader. A look inside the brain explains both why and how.

THE SCIENCE OF MOODS

A growing body of research on the human brain proves that, for better or worse, leaders' moods affect the emotions of the people around them. The reason for that lies in what scientists call the open-loop nature of the brain's limbic system – our emotional center. A closed-loop system is self-regulating, whereas an open-loop system depends on external sources to manage itself. In other words, we rely on connections with other people to determine our moods. The open-loop limbic system was a winning design in evolution because it let people come to one another's emotional rescue – enabling a mother, for example, to soothe her crying infant.

The open-loop design serves the same purpose today as it did thousands of years ago. Research in intensive care units has shown, for example, that the comforting presence of another person not only lowers the patient's blood pressure but also slows the secretion of fatty acids that block arteries. Another study found that three or more incidents of intense stress within a year (for example, serious financial trouble, being fired, or a divorce) triples the death rate in socially isolated middle-aged men, but it has no impact on the death rate of men with many close relationships.

Scientists describe the open-loop as "interpersonal limbic regulation"; one person transmits signals that can alter hormone levels, cardiovascular functions, sleep rhythms, even immune functions, inside the body of another. That's how couples are able to trigger surges of oxytocin in each other's brains, creating a pleasant, affectionate feeling. But in all aspects of social life, our physiologies intermingle. Our limbic system's open-loop design lets other people change our very physiology and hence, our emotions.

Even though the open-loop is so much a part of our lives, we usually don't notice the process. Scientists have captured the attunement of emotions in the laboratory by measuring the physiology – such as heart rate – of two people sharing a good conversation. As the interaction begins, their bodies operate at different rhythms. But after 15 minutes, the physiological profiles of their bodies look remarkably similar.

Researchers have seen again and again how emotions spread irresistibly in this way whenever people are near one another. As far back as 1981, psychologists Howard Friedman and Ronald Riggio found that even completely nonverbal expressiveness can affect other people. For example, when three strangers sit facing one other in silence for a minute or two, the most emotionally expressive of the three transmits his or her mood to the other two – without a single word being spoken.

The same holds true in the office, boardroom, or shop floor; group members inevitably "catch" feelings from one another. In 2000, Caroline Bartel at New York University and Richard Saavedra at the University of Michigan found that in 70 work teams across diverse industries, people in meetings together ended up sharing moods – both good and bad – within two hours. One study asked teams of nurses and accountants to monitor their moods over weeks; researchers discovered that their emotions tracked together, and they were largely independent of each team's shared hassles. Groups, therefore, like individuals, ride emotional rollercoasters, sharing everything from jealousy to angst to euphoria. A good mood, incidentally, spreads most swiftly by the judicious use of humor.

SMILE AND THE WORLD SMILES WITH YOU

Remember that old cliché? It's not too far from the truth. As we've shown, mood contagion is a real neurological phenomenon, but not all emotions spread with the same ease. A 1999 study conducted by Sigal Barsade at the Yale School of Management showed that, among working groups, cheerfulness and warmth spread easily, while irritability caught on less so, and depression least of all.

It should come as no surprise that laughter is the most contagious of emotions. Hearing laughter, we find it almost impossible not to laugh or smile, too. That's because some of our brain's open-loop circuits are designed to detect smiles and laughter, making us respond in kind. Scientists theorize that this dynamic was hardwired into our brains ages ago because smiles and laughter had a way of cementing alliances, thus helping the species survive.

The main implication here for leaders undertaking the primal task of managing their moods and the moods of others is this: Humor hastens the spread of an upbeat climate. But like the leader's mood in general, humor must resonate with the organization's culture and reality. Smiles and laughter, we would posit, are contagious only when they're genuine.

Moods that start at the top tend to move the fastest because everyone watches the boss. They take their emotional cues from him. Even when the boss isn't highly visible – for example, the CEO who works behind closed doors on an upper floor – his attitude affects the moods of his direct reports, and a domino effect ripples throughout the company.

CALL THAT CEO A DOCTOR

If the leader's mood is so important, then he or she had better get into a good one, right? Yes, but the full answer is more complicated than that. A leader's mood has the greatest impact on performance when it is upbeat. But it must also be in tune with those around him. We call this dynamic resonance.

Good moods galvanize good performance, but it doesn't make sense for a leader to be as chipper as a blue jay at dawn if sales are tanking or the business is going under. The most effective executives display moods and behaviors that match the situation at hand, with a healthy dose of optimism mixed in. They respect how other people are feeling – even if it is glum or defeated – but they also model what it looks like to move forward with hope and humor.

This kind of performance, which we call resonance, is for all intents and purposes the four components of emotional intelligence in action.

Self-awareness, perhaps the most essential of the emotional intelligence competencies, is the ability to read your own emotions. It allows people to know their strengths and limitations and feel confident about their self-worth. Resonant leaders use self-awareness to gauge their own moods accurately, and they intuitively know how they are affecting others.

Self-management is the ability to control your emotions and act with honesty and integrity in reliable and adaptable ways. Resonant leaders don't let their occasional bad moods seize the day; they use self-management to leave it outside the office or to explain its source to people in a reasonable manner, so they know where it's coming from and how long it might last.

Social awareness includes the key capabilities of empathy and organizational intuition. Socially aware executives do more than sense other people's emotions; they show that they care. Further, they are experts at reading the currents of office politics. Thus, resonant leaders often keenly understand how their words and actions make others feel, and they are sensitive enough to change them when that impact is negative.

Relationship management, the last of the emotional intelligence competencies, includes the abilities to communicate clearly and convincingly, disarm conflicts, and build strong personal bonds. Resonant leaders use these skills to spread their enthusiasm and solve disagreements, often with humor and kindness.

As effective as resonant leadership is, it is just as rare. Most people suffer through dissonant leaders whose toxic moods and upsetting behaviors wreak havoc before a hopeful and realistic leader repairs the situation.

Consider what happened recently at an experimental division of the BBC, the British media giant. Even though the group's 200 or so journalists and editors had given their best effort, management decided to close the division.

The shutdown itself was bad enough, but the brusque, contentious mood and manner of the executive sent to deliver the news to the assembled staff incited something beyond the expected frustration. People became enraged – at both the decision and the bearer of the news. The executive's cranky mood and delivery created an atmosphere so threatening that he had to call security to be ushered from the room.

The next day, another executive visited the same staff. His mood was somber and respectful, as was his behavior. He spoke about the importance of journalism to the vibrancy of a society and of the calling that had drawn them all to the field in the first place. He reminded them that no one goes into journalism to get rich – as a profession its finances have always been marginal, job security ebbing and flowing with the larger economic tides. He recalled a time in his own career when he had been let go and how he had struggled to find a new position– but how he had stayed dedicated to the profession. Finally, he wished them well in getting on with their careers.

The reaction from what had been an angry mob the day before? When this resonant leader finished speaking, the staff cheered.

We found that an alarming number of leaders do not really know if they have resonance with their organizations. Rather, they suffer from CEO disease; its one unpleasant symptom is the sufferer's near-total ignorance about how his mood and actions appear to the organization. It's not that leaders don't care how they are perceived; most do. But they incorrectly assume that they can decipher this information themselves. Worse, they think that if they are having a negative effect, someone will tell them. They're wrong.

As one CEO in our research explains, "I so often feel I'm not getting the truth. I can never put my finger on it, because no one is actually lying to me. But I can sense that people are hiding information or camouflaging key facts. They aren't lying, but neither are they telling me everything I need to know. I'm always second-guessing."

People don't tell leaders the whole truth about their emotional impact for many reasons. Sometimes they are scared of being the bearer of bad news – and getting shot. Others feel it isn't their place to comment on such a personal topic. Still others don't realize that what they really want to talk about is the effects of the leader's emotional style – that feels too vague. Whatever the reason, the CEO can't rely on his followers to spontaneously give him the full picture.

RESONANCE IN TIMES OF CRISIS

When talking about leaders' moods, the importance of resonance cannot be overstated. While our research suggests that leaders should generally be upbeat, their behavior must be rooted in realism, especially when faced with a crisis.

Consider the response of Bob Mulholland, senior VP and head of the client relations group at Merrill Lynch, to the terrorist attacks in New York. On September 11, 2001, Mulholland and his staff in Two World Financial Center felt the building rock, then watched as smoke poured out of a gaping hole in the building directly across from theirs. People started panicking. Some ran frantically from window to window. Others were paralyzed with fear. Those with relatives working in the World Trade Center were terrified for their safety. Mulholland knew he had to act: "When there's a crisis, you've got to show people the way, step by step, and make sure you're taking care of their concerns."

He started by getting people the information they needed to "unfreeze." He found out, for instance, which floors employees' relatives worked on and assured them that they'd have enough time to escape. Then he calmed the panic-stricken, one at a time. "We're getting out of here now," he said quietly, "and you're coming with me. Not the elevator, take the stairs." He remained calm and decisive, yet he didn't minimize people's emotional responses. Thanks to him, everyone escaped before the towers collapsed.

Mulholland's leadership didn't end there. Recognizing that this event would touch each client personally, he and his team devised a way for financial consultants to connect with their clients on an emotional level. They called every client to ask, "How are you? Are your loved ones okay? How are you feeling?" As Mulholland explains, "There was no way to pick up and do business as usual. The first order of 'business' was letting our clients know we really do care."

Bob Mulholland courageously performed one of the most crucial emotional tasks of leadership: He helped himself and his people find meaning in the face of chaos and madness. To do so, he first attuned to and expressed the shared emotional reality. That's why the direction he eventually articulated resonated on the gut level. His words and his actions reflected what people were feeling in their hearts.

TAKING STOCK

The process we recommend for self-discovery and personal reinvention is neither newfangled nor born of pop psychology, like so many self-help programs offered to executives today. Rather, it is based on three streams of research into how executives can improve the emotional intelligence capabilities most closely linked to effective leadership. In 1989, Richard Boyatzis began drawing on this body of research to design the five-step process itself, and since then, thousands of executives have used it successfully.

Unlike more traditional forms of coaching, our process is based on brain science. A person's emotional skills – the attitude and abilities with which someone approaches life and work – are not genetically hardwired, like eye color and skin tone. But in some ways they might as well be, because they are so deeply embedded in our neurology.

A person's emotional skills do, in fact, have a genetic component. Scientists have discovered, for instance, the gene for shyness – which is not a mood, per se, but it can certainly drive a person toward a persistently quiet demeanor, which may be read as a "down" mood. Other people are preternaturally jolly – that is, their relentless cheerfulness seems preternatural until you meet their peppy parents. As one executive explains, "All I know is that ever since I was a baby, I have always been happy. It drives some people crazy, but I couldn't get blue if I tried. And my brother is the exact same way; he saw the bright side of life, even during his divorce."

Even though emotional skills are partly inborn, experience plays a major role in how the genes are expressed. A happy baby whose parents die or who endures physical abuse may grow into a melancholy adult. A cranky toddler may turn into a cheerful adult after discovering a fulfilling avocation. Still, research suggests that our range of emotional skills is relatively set by our mid-20s and that our accompanying behaviors are, by that time, deep-seated habits. And therein lies the rub: The more we act a certain way – be it happy, depressed, or cranky – the more the behavior becomes ingrained in our brain circuitry, and the more we will continue to feel and act that way. That's why emotional intelligence matters so much for a leader. An emotionally intelligent leader can monitor his or her moods through self-awareness, change them for the better through self-management, understand their impact through empathy, and act in ways that boost others' moods through relationship management.

The following five-part process is designed to rewire the brain toward more emotionally intelligent behaviors. The process begins with imagining your ideal self and then coming to terms with your real self, as others experience you. The next step is creating a tactical plan to bridge the gap between ideal and real, and after that, to practice those activities. It concludes with creating a community of colleagues and family – call them change enforcers – to keep the process alive. Let's look at the steps in more detail.

"Who do I want to be?" Sofia, a senior manager at a northern European telecommunications company, knew she needed to understand how her emotional leadership affected others. Whenever she felt stressed, she tended to communicate poorly and take over subordinates' work so that the job would be done "right." Attending leadership seminars hadn't changed her habits, and neither had reading management books or working with mentors.

When Sofia came to us, we asked her to imagine herself eight years from now as an effective leader and to write a description of a typical day. "What would she be doing?" we asked. "Where would she live? Who would be there? How would it feel?" We urged her to consider her deepest values and loftiest dreams and to explain how those ideals had become a part of her everyday life.

Sofia pictured herself leading her own tight-knit company staffed by ten colleagues. She was enjoying an open relationship with her daughter and had trusting relationships with her friends and coworkers. She saw herself as a relaxed and happy leader and parent and as loving and empowering to all those around her.

In general, Sofia had a low level of self-awareness. She was rarely able to pinpoint why she was struggling at work and at home. All she could say was, "Nothing is working right." This exercise, which prompted her to picture what life would look like if everything were going right, opened her eyes to the missing elements in her emotional style. She was able to see the impact she had on people in her life.

"Who am I now?" In the next step of the discovery process, you come to see your leadership style as others do. This is both difficult and dangerous. Difficult, because few people have the guts to tell the boss or a colleague what he's really like. And dangerous, because such information can sting or even paralyze. A small bit of ignorance about yourself isn't always a bad thing: Ego-defense mechanisms have their advantages. Research by Martin Seligman shows that high-functioning people generally feel more optimistic about their prospects and possibilities than average performers. Their rose-colored lenses, in fact, fuel the enthusiasm and energy that make the unexpected and the extraordinary achievable. Playwright Henrik Ibsen called such self-delusions "vital lies," soothing mistruths we let ourselves believe in order to face a daunting world.

But self-delusion should come in very small doses. Executives should relentlessly seek the truth about themselves, especially since it is sure to be somewhat diluted when they hear it anyway. One way to get the truth is to keep an extremely open attitude toward critiques. Another is to seek out negative feedback, even cultivating a colleague or two to play devil's advocate.

We also highly recommend gathering feedback from as many people as possible – including bosses, peers, and subordinates. Feedback from subordinates and peers is especially helpful because it most accurately predicts a leader's effectiveness, two, four, and even seven years out, according to research by Glenn McEvoy at Utah State and Richard Beatty at Rutgers University.

Of course, 360-degree feedback doesn't specifically ask people to evaluate your moods, actions, and their impact. But it does reveal how people experience you. For instance, when people rate how well you listen, they are really reporting how well they think you hear them. Similarly, when 360-degree feedback elicits ratings about coaching effectiveness, the answers show whether or not people feel you understand and care about them. When the feedback uncovers low scores on, say, openness to new ideas, it means that people experience you as inaccessible or unapproachable or both. In sum, all you need to know about your emotional impact is in 360-degree feedback, if you look for it.

One last note on this second step. It is, of course, crucial to identify your areas of weakness. But focusing only on your weaknesses can be dispiriting. That's why it is just as important, maybe even more so, to understand your strengths. Knowing where your real self overlaps with your ideal self will give you the positive energy you need to move forward to the next step in the process – bridging the gaps.

"How do I get from here to there?" Once you know who you want to be and have compared it with how people see you, you need to devise an action plan. For Sofia, this meant planning for a real improvement in her level of self-awareness. So she asked each member of her team at work to give her feedback – weekly, anonymously, and in written form – about her mood and performance and their affect on people. She also committed herself to three tough but achievable tasks: spending an hour each day reflecting on her behavior in a journal, taking a class on group dynamics at a local college, and enlisting the help of a trusted colleague as an informal coach.

Consider, too, how Juan, a marketing executive for the Latin American division of a major integrated energy company, completed this step. Juan was charged with growing the company in his home country of Venezuela as well as in the entire region – a job that would require him to be a coach and a visionary and to have an encouraging, optimistic outlook. Yet 360-degree feedback revealed that Juan was seen as intimidating and internally focused. Many of his direct reports saw him as a grouch – impossible to please at his worst, and emotionally draining at his best. Identifying this gap allowed Juan to craft a plan with manageable steps toward improvement. He knew he needed to hone his powers of empathy if he wanted to develop a coaching style, so he committed to various activities that would let him practice that skill. For instance,

Juan decided to get to know each of his subordinates better; if he understood more about who they were, he thought, he'd be more able to help them reach their goals. He made plans with each employee to meet outside of work, where they might be more comfortable revealing their feelings.

Juan also looked for areas outside of his job to forge his missing links – for example, coaching his daughter's soccer team and volunteering at a local crisis center. Both activities helped him to experiment with how well he understood others and to try out new behaviors.

Again, let's look at the brain science at work. Juan was trying to overcome ingrained behaviors – his approach to work had taken hold overtime, without his realizing it. Bringing them into awareness was a crucial step toward changing them. As he paid more attention, the situations that arose – while listening to a colleague, coaching soccer, or talking on the phone to someone who was distraught – all became cues that stimulated him to break old habits and try new responses.

This cueing for habit change is neural as well as perceptual. Researchers at the University of Pittsburgh and Carnegie Mellon University have shown that as we mentally prepare for a task, we activate the prefrontal cortex – the part of the brain that moves us into action. The greater the prior activation, the better we do at the task.

Such mental preparation becomes particularly important when we're trying to replace an old habit with a better one. As neuroscientist Cameron Carter at the University of Pittsburgh found, the prefrontal cortex becomes particularly active when a person prepares to overcome a habitual response. The aroused prefrontal cortex marks the brain's focus on what's about to happen. Without that arousal, a person will reenact tried-and-true but undesirable routines. The executive who just doesn't listen will once again cut off his subordinate, a ruthless leader will launch into yet another critical attack, and so on. That's why a learning agenda is so important. Without one, we literally do not have the brainpower to change.

"How do I make change stick?" In short, making change last requires practice. The reason, again, lies in the brain. It takes doing and redoing, over and over, to break old neural habits. A leader must rehearse a new behavior until it becomes automatic – that is, until he's mastered it at the level of implicit learning. Only then will the new wiring replace the old.

While it is best to practice new behaviors, as Juan did, sometimes just envisioning them will do. Take the case of Tom, an executive who wanted to close the gap between his real self (perceived by colleagues and subordinates to be cold and hard driving) and his ideal self (a visionary and a coach).

Tom's learning plan involved finding opportunities to step back and coach his employees rather than jumping down their throats when he sensed they were wrong. Tom also began to spend idle moments during his commute thinking through how to handle encounters he would have that day. One morning, while en route to a breakfast meeting with an employee who seemed to be bungling a project, Tom ran through a positive scenario in his mind. He asked questions and listened to be sure he fully understood the situation before trying to solve the problem. He anticipated feeling impatient, and he rehearsed how he would handle these feelings.

Studies on the brain affirm the benefits of Tom's visualization technique: Imagining something in vivid detail can fire the same brain cells actually involved in doing that activity. The new brain circuitry appears to go through its paces, strengthening connections, even when we merely repeat the sequence in our minds. So to alleviate the fears associated with trying out riskier ways of leading, we should first visualize some likely scenarios. Doing so will make us feel less awkward when we actually put the new skills into practice.

Experimenting with new behaviors and seizing opportunities inside and outside of work to practice them – as well as using such methods as mental rehearsal – eventually triggers in our brains the neural connections necessary for genuine change to occur. Even so, lasting change doesn't happen through experimentation and brain-power alone. We need, as the song goes, a little help from our friends.

"Who can help me?" The fifth step in the self-discovery and reinvention process is creating a community of supporters. Take, for example, managers at Unilever who formed learning groups as part of their executive development process. At first, they gathered to discuss their careers and how to provide leadership. But because they were also charged with discussing their dreams and their learning goals, they soon realized that they were discussing both their work and their personal lives. They developed a strong mutual trust and began relying on one another for frank feedback as they worked on strengthening their leadership abilities. When this happens, the business benefits through stronger performance. Many professionals today have created similar groups, and for good reason. People we trust let us try out unfamiliar parts of our leadership repertoire without risk.

We cannot improve our emotional intelligence or change our leadership style without help from others. We not only practice with other people, but also rely on them to create a safe environment in which to experiment. We need to get feedback about how our actions affect others and to assess our progress on our learning agenda.

In fact, perhaps paradoxically, in the self-directed learning process we draw on others every step of the way – from articulating and refining our ideal self and comparing it with the reality to the final assessment that affirms our progress. Our relationships offer us the very context in which we understand our progress and comprehend the usefulness of what we're learning.

MOOD OVER MATTER

When we say that managing your mood and the moods of your followers is the task of primal leadership, we certainly don't mean to suggest that mood is all that matters.

As we've noted, your actions are critical, and mood and actions together must resonate with the organization and with reality. Similarly, we acknowledge all the other challenges leaders must conquer – from strategy to hiring to new product development. It's all in a long day's work.

But taken as a whole, the message sent by neurological, psychological, and organizational research is startling in its clarity. Emotional leadership is the spark that ignites a company's performance, creating a bonfire of success or a landscape of ashes. Moods matter that much.

POSTSCRIPT

Originally Published on hbr.com
and LinkedIn.com

WHEN YOU CRITICIZE SOMEONE YOU MAKE IT HARDER FOR THEM TO CHANGE

hbr.com - December 19, 2013

"If everything worked out perfectly in your life, what would you be doing in ten years?"

Such a question opens us up to fresh possibilities, to reflect on what matters most to us, and even what deep values might guide us through life. This approach gives managers a tool for coaching their teams to get better results.

Contrast that mind-opening query with a conversation about what's wrong with you, and what you need to do to fix yourself. That line of thinking shuts us down, puts us on the defensive, and narrows our possibilities to rescue operations. Managers should keep this in mind, particularly during performance reviews.

That question about your perfect life

in ten years comes from Richard Boyatzis, a professor at the Weatherhead School of Management at Case Western, and an old friend and colleague. His recent research on the best approach to coaching has used brain imaging to analyze how coaching affects the brain differently when you focus on dreams instead of failings. These findings have great implications for how to best help someone – or yourself – improve.

As I quoted Boyatzis in my book *Focus: The Hidden Driver of Excellence*, "Talking about your positive goals and dreams activates brain centers that open you up to new possibilities. But if you change the conversation to what you should do to fix yourself, it closes you down."

Working with colleagues at Cleveland Clinic, Boyatzis put people through a positive, dreams-first interview or a negative, problems-focused one while their brains were scanned. The positive interview elicited activity in reward circuitry and areas for good memories and upbeat feelings – a brain signature of the open hopefulness we feel when embracing an inspiring vision. In contrast, the negative interview activated brain circuitry for anxiety, the same areas that activate when we feel sad and worried. In the latter state, the anxiety and defensiveness elicited make it more difficult to focus on the possibilities for improvement.

Of course a manager needs to help

people face what's not working. As Boyatzis put it, "You need the negative focus to survive, but a positive one to thrive. You need both, but in the right ratio."

Barbara Frederickson, a psychologist at the University of North Carolina, finds that positive feelings enlarge the aperture of our attention to embrace a wider range of possibility and to motivate us to work toward a better future. She finds that people who do well in their private and work lives alike generally have a higher ratio of positive states to negative ones during their day.

Being in the positive mood range activates brain circuits that remind us of how good we will feel when we reach a goal, according to research by Richard Davidson at the University of Wisconsin. That's the circuit that keeps us working away at the small steps we need to take toward a larger goal – whether finishing a major project or a change in our own behavior.

This brain circuitry – vital for working toward our goals – runs on dopamine, a feel-good brain chemical, along with endogenous opioids like endorphins, the "runner's high" neurotransmitters. This chemical brew fuels drive and tags it with satisfying dollops of pleasure. That may be why maintaining a positive view pays off for performance, as Frederickson's research has found: it energizes us, lets us focus better, be more flexible in our thinking, and connect effectively with the people around us.

Managers and coaches can keep this in mind. Boyatzis makes the case that understanding a person's dreams can open a conversation about what it would take to fulfill those hopes. And that can lead to concrete learning goals. Often those goals are improving capacities like conscientiousness, listening, collaboration and the like – which can yield better performance.

Boyatzis tells of an executive MBA student, a manager who wanted to build better work relationships. The manager had an engineering background; when it came to getting a task done, "all he saw was the task," says Boyatzis, "not the people he worked with to get it done."

His learning curve involved tuning in to how other people felt. For a low-risk chance to practice this he took on coaching his son's soccer team – and making the effort to notice how team members felt as he coached them. That became a habit he took back to work.

By starting with the positive goal he wanted to achieve – richer work relationships – rather than framing it as a personal flaw he wanted to overcome, he made achieving his goal that much easier.

Bottom line: don't focus on only on weaknesses, but on hopes and dreams. It's what our brains are wired to do.

THE SIGNS OF A LEADER'S EMPATHY DEFICIT DISORDER

linkedin.com - November 25, 2013

Think of two people who work in your organization: one a level or two below you, and the other a level above. Now imagine getting an email from each of them. Ask yourself how long it would take you to answer those emails.

Chances are the one from above you respond to right away. And the one from below you are likely to answer when you can get around to it.

That difference in response times has been used to map the hierarchy in an organization. And it reflects a more general principle: we pay more attention to those who hold more power than we do – and notice less those who hold less power.

The relationship between power and focus shows up starkly in interactions as simple as two strangers meeting for the first time. In just five minutes of conversation, the person of higher social status generally gives fewer indicators of attention, like eye contact and nods than does the one who holds less social power. This attention gap has even surfaced even among college students from wealthier and poorer families.

That analysis of response times to email was done using the entire email database of Enron Corporation, which became available to researchers after it was used to investigate the firm's collapse. The program for detecting the social networks in an organization through email analysis was developed at Columbia University, and proved remarkably accurate.

When attention flows along power lines, empathy also takes a hit. When strangers told each other about divorces or other painful moments in their lives, there was more empathy expressed by the less powerful person. Another measure of empathy – the accuracy with which we can tell a person's feelings from clues like facial expression – also turns out to differ, with lower status people more skilled than those of higher positions.

This fact of social life poses a danger for leaders – after all, the most effective leaders are outstanding at abilities that build on empathy, like persuasion and influence, motivating and listening, teamwork and collaboration.

There are three kinds of empathy. First, cognitive, where you sense how the other person thinks about the world, which means you can put what you have to say in terms they will understand. Second, emotional, where you instantly resonate with how the person feels. And third, empathic concern, where you express the ways you care about the person by helping with what you sense they need.

The signs of a leadership empathy deficit in any or all of these varieties can best be detected by how a leader's actions impact those he or she leads. Some of the common signs are:

- Directives or memos that make no sense to those receiving them are a sign that a boss does not understand how employees think about their world, and fails to tune in to the language that would make most sense to them. Another sign of low cognitive empathy: strategies, plans or goals that make little sense or seem off-point to those who are to execute them.

- Communiqués or, worse, commands, that upset those receiving them. This signifies a boss who doesn't accurately read the emotional reality of employees, and so seems clueless to those receiving them.

- Expressing attitudes that seem cold or just out-of-touch with the issues employees struggle with signifies a lack of empathic concern. Feeling your boss doesn't care puts employees on the defensive, where they are afraid to take risks like innovating.

Leaders at higher levels are perhaps most in danger of coming down with empathy deficit disorder, for a simple reason: as you rise through the ranks fewer and fewer people are candid with you, willing to give you frank feedback on how you seem to others.

Among the ways to prevent an empathy deficit might be joining what Harvard Business School's Bill George calls "true north groups," where you get honest feedback from people who know you well. Another might be creating an informal network of colleagues who will be frank with you (perhaps outside your organization) and staying in regular touch with them – or the same with trusted friends at all levels within your own firm.

High-contact leaders, who wander around and spend informal time getting to know employees, inoculate themselves against empathy deficit. The same goes for leaders who create a workplace atmosphere where people feel safe being candid – including with the boss.

REAWAKENING YOUR PASSION FOR WORK

written with Richard Boyatzis
and Annie McKee

Originally published in the Harvard Business
Review, April 2002

On September 11, 2001, as millions
of people around the globe stared in disbelief
at television screens, watching the World Trade
Center towers crumble to the ground, many of us
realized that accompanying the shock and sorrow
was another sensation – the impulse to take stock.
The fragile nature of human life, exposed with
such unbearable clarity, compelled people to ask a
haunting question: "Am I really living the way I want
to live?"

We all struggle with the question of
personal meaning throughout our lives. September
11th brought the issue into focus for many people
all at once, but the impulse to take stock comes
up periodically for most of us in far less dramatic
circumstances. Senior executives, for instance,
seem to struggle with this question at the high point
of their careers. Why? Many executives hit their

professional stride in their forties and fifties, just as their parents are reaching the end of their lives – a reminder that all of us are mortal. What's more, many of the personality traits associated with career success, such as a knack for problem solving and sheer tenacity, lead people to stick with a difficult situation in the hope of making it better. Then one day, a creeping sensation sets in: Something is wrong. That realization launches a process we have witnessed literally thousands of times in our work coaching managers and executives over the past 14 years.

The process is rarely easy, but we've found this type of awakening to be healthy and necessary; leaders need to go through it every few years to replenish their energy, creativity, and commitment – and to rediscover their passion for work and life. Indeed, leaders cannot keep achieving new goals and inspiring the people around them without understanding their own dreams. In this article, we'll look at the different signals that it's time to take stock – whether you have a nagging sense of doubt that builds over time until it's impossible to ignore or you experience a life-changing event that irrevocably alters your perspective. Then we'll describe some strategies for listening to those signals and taking restorative action. Such action can range from a relatively minor adjustment in outlook, to a larger refocusing on what really matters, to practical life changes that take you in an entirely new direction.

WHEN TO SAY WHEN

When asked, most businesspeople say that passion – to lead, to serve the customer, to support a cause or a product – is what drives them. When that passion fades, they begin to question the meaning of their work. How can you reawaken the passion and reconnect with what's meaningful for you? The first step is acknowledging the signal that it's time to take stock. Let's look at the various feelings that let you know the time has come.

"I feel trapped."

Sometimes, a job that was fulfilling gradually becomes less meaningful, slowly eroding your enthusiasm and spirit until you no longer find much purpose in your work. People often describe this state as feeling trapped. They're restless, yet they can't seem to change – or even articulate what's wrong.

Take the case of Bob McDowell, the corporate director of human resources at a large professional-services firm. After pouring his heart and soul into his work for 25 years, Bob had become terribly demoralized because his innovative programs were cut time and again. As a result, his efforts could do little to improve the workplace over the long term. For years he had quieted his nagging doubts, in part because an occasional success or a rare employee who flourished under his guidance provided deep, if temporary, satisfaction. Moreover, the job carried all the usual trappings of success – title, money, and perks. And, like most people in middle age, McDowell had financial responsibilities that made it risky to trade security for personal fulfillment. Factors such as these conspire to keep people trudging along, hoping things will get better. But clinging to security or trying to be a good corporate citizen can turn out to be a prison of your own making.

"I'm bored."

Many people confuse achieving day-to-day business goals with performing truly satisfying work, so they continue setting and achieving new goals – until it dawns on them that they are bored. People are often truly shaken by this revelation; they feel as if they have just emerged from a spiritual blackout. We saw this in Nick Mimken, the owner of a successful insurance agency, who increasingly felt that something was missing from his life. He joined a book group, hoping that intellectual stimulation would help him regain some enthusiasm, but it wasn't enough. The fact was, he had lost touch with his dreams and was going through the motions at work without experiencing any real satisfaction from the success of his business.

High achievers like Mimken may have trouble accepting that they're bored because it's often the generally positive traits of ambition and determination to succeed that obscure the need for fun. Some people may feel guilty about being restless when it looks like they have it all. Others may admit they aren't having fun but believe that's the price of success. As one manager said, "I work to live. I don't expect to find deep meaning at the office; I get that elsewhere." The problem? Like many, this man works more than 60 hours a week, leaving him little time to enjoy anything else.

"I'm not the person I want to be."

Some people gradually adjust to the letdowns, frustrations, and even boredom of their work until they surrender to a routine that's incompatible with who they are and what they truly want. Consider, for instance, John Lauer, an inspirational leader who took over as president of BFGoodrich and quickly captured the support of top executives with his insight into the company's challenges and opportunities, and his contagious passion for the business.

But after he'd been with the company about six years, we watched Lauer give a speech to a class of executive MBA students and saw that he had lost his spark. Over time, Lauer had fallen in step with a corporate culture that was focused on shareholder value in a way that was inconsistent with what he cared about. Not surprisingly, he left the company six months later, breaking from corporate life by joining his wife in her work with Hungarian relief organizations. He later admitted that he knew he wasn't himself by the end of his time at BFGoodrich, although he didn't quite know why.

How did Lauer stray from his core? First, the change was so gradual that he didn't notice that he was being absorbed into a culture that didn't fit him. Second, like many, he did what he felt he "should," going along with the bureaucracy and making minor concession after minor concession rather than following his heart. Finally, he exhibited a trait that is a hallmark of effective leaders: adaptability. At first, adapting to the corporate culture probably made Lauer feel more comfortable. But without strong self-awareness, people risk adapting to such an extent that they no longer recognize themselves.

"I won't compromise my ethics."

The signal to take stock may come to people in the form of a challenge to what they feel is right. Such was the case for Niall FitzGerald, now the cochairman of Unilever, when he was asked to take a leadership role in South Africa, which was still operating under apartheid. The offer was widely considered a feather in his cap and a positive sign about his future with Unilever. Until that time, FitzGerald had accepted nearly every assignment, but the South Africa opportunity stopped him in his tracks, posing a direct challenge to his principles. How could he, in good conscience, accept a job in a country whose political and practical environment he found reprehensible?

Or consider the case of a manager we'll call Rob. After working for several supportive and loyal bosses, he found himself reporting to an executive – we'll call him Martin – whose management style was in direct conflict with Rob's values. The man's abusive treatment of subordinates had derailed a number of promising careers, yet he was something of a legend in the company. To Rob's chagrin, the senior executive team admired Martin's performance and, frankly, felt that young managers benefited from a stint under his marine lieutenant–style leadership.

When you recognize that an experience is in conflict with your values, as FitzGerald and Rob did, you can at least make a conscious choice about how to respond. The problem is, people often miss this particular signal because they lose sight of their core values. Sometimes they separate their work from their personal lives to such an extent that they don't bring their values to the office. As a result, they may accept or even engage in behaviors they'd deem unacceptable at home. Other people find that their work becomes their life, and business goals take precedence over everything else. Many executives who genuinely value family above all still end up working 12-hour days, missing more and more family dinners as they pursue success at work. In these cases, people may not hear the wake-up call. Even if they do, they may sense that something isn't quite right but be unable to identify it – or do anything to change it.

"I can't ignore the call."

A wake-up call can come in the form of a mission: an irresistible force that compels people to step out, step up, and take on a challenge. It is as if they suddenly recognize what they are meant to do and cannot ignore it any longer.

Such a call is often spiritual, as in the case of the executive who, after examining his values and personal vision, decided to quit his job, become ordained, buy a building, and start a church – all at age 55. But a call can take other forms as well – to become a teacher, to work with disadvantaged children, or to make a difference to the people you encounter every day. Rebecca Yoon, who runs a dry-cleaning business, has come to consider it her mission to connect with her customers on a personal level. Her constant and sincere attention has created remarkable loyalty to her shop, even though the actual service she provides is identical to that delivered by hundreds of other dry cleaners in the city.

"Life is too short!"

Sometimes it takes a trauma, large or small, to jolt people into taking a hard look at their lives. Such an awakening may be the result of a heart attack, the loss of a loved one, or a world tragedy. It can also be the result of something less dramatic, like adjusting to an empty nest or celebrating a significant birthday. Priorities can become crystal clear at times like these, and things that seemed important weeks, days, or even minutes ago no longer matter.

For example, following a grueling and heroic escape from his office at One World Trade Center on September 11th, John Paul DeVito of the May Davis Group stumbled into a church in tears, desperate to call his family. When a police officer tried to calm him down, DeVito responded, "I'm not in shock. I've never been more cognizant in my life." Even as he mourned the deaths of friends and colleagues, he continued to be ecstatic about life, and he's now reframing his priorities, amazed that before this horrific experience he put duty to his job above almost everything else.

DeVito is not alone. Anecdotal evidence suggests that many people felt the need to seek new meaning in their lives after the tragedies of September 11th, which highlighted the fact that life can be cut short at any time. An article in the December 26, 2001, *Wall Street Journal* described two women who made dramatic changes after the attacks. Following a visit to New York shortly after the towers were hit, engineer Betty Roberts quit her job at age 52 to enroll in divinity school. And Chicki Wentworth decided to give up the office and restaurant building she had owned and managed for nearly 30 years in order to work with troubled teens.

But as we've said, people also confront awakening events throughout their lives in much more mundane circumstances. Turning 40, getting married, sending a child to college, undergoing surgery, facing retirement – these are just a handful of the moments in life when we naturally pause, consider where our choices have taken us, and check our accomplishments against our dreams.

Interestingly, it's somehow more socially acceptable to respond to shocking or traumatic events than to any of the others. As a result, people who feel trapped and bored often stick with a job that's making them miserable for far too long, and thus they may be more susceptible to stress-related illnesses. What's more, the quieter signals – a sense of unease that builds over time, for example – can be easy to miss or dismiss because their day-to-day impact is incremental. But such signals are no less important as indicators of the need to reassess than the more visible events. How do you learn to listen to vital signals and respond before it's too late? It takes a conscious, disciplined effort at periodic self-examination.

STRATEGIES FOR RENEWAL

There's no one-size-fits-all solution for restoring meaning and passion to your life. However, there are strategies for assessing your life and making corrections if you've gotten off course. Most people pursue not a single strategy but a combination, and some seek outside help while others prefer a more solitary journey. Regardless of which path you choose, you need time for reflection – a chance to consider where you are, where you're going, and where you really want to be. Let's look at five approaches.

Call a time-out
For some people, taking time off is the best way to figure out what they really want to do and to reconnect with their dreams. Academic institutions have long provided time for rejuvenation through sabbaticals – six to 12 months off, often with pay. Some businesses – to be clear, very few – offer sabbaticals as well, letting people take a paid leave to pursue their interests with the guarantee of a job when they return. More often, businesspeople who take time off do so on their own time – a risk, to be sure, but few who have stepped off the track regret the decision.

This is the path Bob McDowell took. McDowell, the HR director we described earlier who felt trapped in his job, stepped down from his position, did not look for another job, and spent about eight months taking stock of his life. He considered his successes and failures, and faced up to the sacrifices he had made by dedicating himself so completely to a job that was, in the end, less than fulfilling. Other executives take time off with far less ambitious goals – simply to get their heads out of their work for a while and focus on their personal lives. After a time, they may very happily go back to the work they'd been doing for years, eager to embrace the same challenges with renewed passion.

Still others might want to step off the fast track and give their minds a rest by doing something different. When Nick Mimken, the bored head of an insurance agency, took stock of his life and finally realized he wasn't inspired by his work, he decided to sell his business, keep only a few clients, and take sculpture classes. He then went to work as a day laborer for a landscaper in order to pursue his interest in outdoor sculpture – in particular, stone fountains. Today he and his wife live in Nantucket, Massachusetts, where he no longer works for a living but at living. He is exploring what speaks to him – be it rock sculpture, bronze casting, protecting wildlife, or teaching people how to handle their money. Nick is deeply passionate about his work and how he is living his life. He calls himself a life explorer.

In any event, whether it's an intense, soul-searching exercise or simply a break from corporate life, people almost invariably find time-outs energizing. But stepping out isn't easy. No to-do list, no meetings or phone calls, no structure – it can be difficult for high achievers to abandon their routines. The loss of financial security makes this move inconceivable for some. And for the many people whose identities are tied up in their professional lives, walking away feels like too great a sacrifice. Indeed, we've seen people jump back onto the train within a week or two without reaping any benefit from the time off, just because they could not stand to be away from work.

Find a program
While a time-out can be little more than a refreshing pause, a leadership or executive development program is a more structured strategy, guiding people as they explore their dreams and open new doors.

Remember John Lauer? Two years after Lauer left BFGoodrich, he was still working with Hungarian refugees (his time-out) and maintained that he wanted nothing to do with running a company. Yet as part of his search for the next phase of his career, he decided to pursue an executive doctorate degree. While in the program, he took a leadership development seminar in which a series of exercises forced him to clarify his values, philosophy, aspirations, and strengths.

TOOLS FOR REFLECTION

Once you've lost touch with your passion and dreams, the very routine of work and the habits of your mind can make it difficult to reconnect. Here are some tools that can help people break from those routines and allow their dreams to come to the surface again.

Reflecting on the Past

Alone and with trusted friends and advisers, periodically do a reality check. Take an hour or two and draw your "lifeline." Beginning with childhood, plot the high points and the low points – the events that caused you great joy and great sorrow. Note the times you were most proud, most excited, and most strong and clear. Note also the times you felt lost and alone. Point out for yourself the transitions – times when things fundamentally changed for you. Now, look at the whole. What are some of the underlying themes? What seems to be ever present, no matter the situation? What values seem to weigh in most often and most heavily when you make changes in your life? Are you generally on a positive track, or have there been lots of ups and downs? Where does luck or fate fit in?

Now, switch to the more recent past and consider these questions: What has or has not changed at work, in life? How am I feeling? How do I see myself these days? Am I living my values? Am I having fun? Do my values still fit with what I need to do at work and with what my company is doing? Have my dreams changed? Do I still believe in my vision of my future?

As a way to pull it all together, do a bit of free-form writing, finishing the sentence: "In my life I... and now I... "

Defining Your Principles for Life

Think about the different aspects of your life that are important, such as family, relationships, work, spirituality, and physical health. What are your core values in each of those areas? List five or six principles that guide you in life and think about whether they are values that you truly live by or simply talk about.

Extending the Horizon

Try writing a page or two about what you would like to do with the rest of your life. Or you might want to number a sheet of paper 1 through 27 and then list all the things you want to do or experience before you die. Don't feel the need to stop at 27, and don't worry about priorities or practicality – just write down whatever comes to you.

This exercise is harder than it seems because it's human nature to think more in terms of what we have to do – by tomorrow, next week, or next month. But with such a short horizon, we can focus only on what's urgent, not on what's important. When we think in terms of the extended horizon, such as what we might do before we die, we open up a new range of possibilities. In our work with leaders who perform this exercise, we've seen a surprising trend: Most people jot down a few career goals, but 80% or more of their lists have nothing to do with work. When they finish the exercise and study their writing, they see patterns that help them begin to crystallize their dreams and aspirations.

Envisioning the Future
Think about where you would be sitting and reading this article if it were 15 years from now and you were living your ideal life. What kinds of people would be around you? How would your environment look and feel? What might you be doing during a typical day or week? Don't worry about the feasibility of creating this life; rather, let the image develop and place yourself in the picture.

Try doing some free-form writing about this vision of yourself, speak your vision into a tape recorder, or talk about it with a trusted friend. Many people report that, when doing this exercise, they experience a release of energy and feel more optimistic than they had even moments earlier. Envisioning an ideal future can be a powerful way to connect with the possibilities for change in our lives.

In considering the next decade of his life and reflecting on his capabilities, Lauer realized that his resistance to running a company actually represented a fear of replicating his experience at BFGoodrich. In fact, he loved being at the helm of an organization where he could convey his vision and lead the company forward, and he relished working with a team of like-minded executives. Suddenly, he realized that he missed those aspects of the CEO job and that in the right kind of situation – one in which he could apply the ideas he'd developed in his studies – being a CEO could be fun.

With this renewed passion to lead, Lauer returned a few headhunters' calls and within a month was offered the job of chairman and CEO at Oglebay Norton, a $250 million company in the raw-materials business. There he became an exemplar of the democratic leadership style, welcoming employees' input and encouraging his leadership team to do the same. As one of his executives told us, "John raises our spirits, our confidence, and our passion for excellence." Although the company deals in such unglamorous commodities as gravel and sand, Lauer made so many improvements in his first year that Oglebay Norton was featured in Fortune, Business Week, and the Wall Street Journal.

Another executive we know, Tim Schramko, had a long career managing health care companies. As a diversion, he began teaching part-time. He took on a growing course load while fulfilling his business responsibilities, but he was running himself ragged. It wasn't until he went through a structured process to help him design his ideal future that he realized he had a calling to teach. Once that was clear, he developed a plan for extricating himself from his business obligations over a two-year period and is now a full-time faculty member.

Many educational institutions offer programs that support this type of move. What's more, some companies have developed their own programs in the realization that leaders who have a chance to reconnect with their dreams tend to return with redoubled energy and commitment. The risk, of course, is that after serious reflection, participants will jump ship. But in our experience, most find new meaning and passion in their current positions. In any event, people who do leave weren't in the right job – and they would have realized it sooner or later.

Create "Reflective Structures"

When leadership guru Warren Bennis interviewed leaders from all walks of life in the early 1990s, he found that they had a common way of staying in touch with what was important to them. They built into their lives what Bennis calls "reflective structures": time and space for self-examination, whether a few hours a week, a day or two a month, or a longer period every year.

For many people, religious practices provide an outlet for reflection, and some people build time into the day or week for prayer or meditation. But reflection does not have to involve organized religion. Exercise is an outlet for many people, and some executives set aside time in their calendars for regular workouts. One CEO of a $2 billion utility company reserves eight hours a week for solitary reflection – an hour a day, perhaps two or three hours on a weekend. During that time, he might go for a long walk, work in his home shop, or take a ride on his Harley. However you spend the time, the idea is to get away from the demands of your job and be with your own thoughts.

Increasingly, we've seen people seek opportunities for collective reflection as well, so that they can share their dreams and frustrations with their peers. On his third time heading a major division of the Hay Group, Murray Dalziel decided to build some reflection into his life by joining a CEO group that meets once a month. In a sense, the group legitimizes time spent thinking, talking, and learning from one another. Members have created a trusting community where they can share honest feedback – a scarce resource for most executives. And all gain tangible benefits; people exchange tips on how to fix broken processes or navigate sticky situations.

Work With a Coach

Our own biases and experiences sometimes make it impossible for us to find a way out of a difficult or confusing situation; we need an outside perspective. Help can come informally from family, friends, and colleagues, or it can come from a professional coach skilled at helping people see their strengths and identify new ways to use them. We won't discuss more traditional therapy in this article, but it is, of course, another alternative.

When Bob McDowell, the HR director, stepped out of his career, he sought out a variety of personal and professional connections to help him decide how to approach the future. Working with an executive coach, McDowell was able to identify what was important to him in life and translate that to what he found essential in a job. He could then draw clear lines around the aspects of his personal life he would no longer compromise, including health and exercise, time with his family, personal hobbies, and other interests. In the end, he found his way to a new career as a partner in an executive search business – a job he'd never considered but one that matched his passion for helping people and the companies they work for. What's more, his soul-searching had so sparked his creativity that in his new position he combined traditional organizational consulting with the search process to discover unusual possibilities. Instead of a typical executive search, he helps companies find employees who will bring magic to the business and to the relationships essential to success.

What did the coach bring to McDowell's self-reflection? Perhaps the chief benefit was a trusting, confidential relationship that gave him the space to dream – something executives shy away from, largely because the expectations of society and their families weigh on them so heavily. Like many, McDowell began this process assuming that he would simply narrow his priorities, clarify his work goals, and chart a new professional path. But to his surprise, his coach's perspective helped him see new opportunities in every part of his life, not just in his work.

Sometimes, however, the coach does little more than help you recognize what you already know at some level. Richard Whiteley, the cofounder of a successful international consulting firm and author of several business best-sellers, felt that he wasn't having as much fun as he used to; he was restless and wanted a change. To that end, he began to do some work on the side, helping business-people improve their effectiveness through spiritual development. He was considering leaving his consulting practice behind altogether and concentrating on the spiritual work – but he was torn. He turned to a spiritual leader, who told him, "Forget the spiritual work and concentrate on the work you've been doing." Only when forced to choose the wrong path could Richard recognize what he truly wanted to do. Within a few months, Richard had devoted himself to writing and speaking almost exclusively on spirituality and passion in work – and he's thriving.

Find New Meaning in Familiar Territory

It's not always feasible to change your job or move somewhere new, even if your situation is undesirable. And frankly, many people don't want to make such major changes. But it is often easier than you might think to make small adjustments so that your work more directly reflects your beliefs and values – as long as you know what you need and have the courage to take some risks.

Back to Niall FitzGerald, who was confronted with the decision over whether to live and work in South Africa. A strong and principled person as well as a good corporate citizen, FitzGerald eventually decided to break with company culture by accepting the job on one unprecedented condition: If over the first six months or so he found his involvement with the country intolerable, he would be allowed to take another job at Unilever, no questions asked. He then set forth to find ways to exert a positive influence on his new work environment wherever possible.

As the leader of a prominent business, FitzGerald had some clout, of course, but he knew that he could not take on the government directly. His response: Figure out what he could change, do it, and then deal with the system. For example, when he was building a new plant, the architect showed FitzGerald plans with eight bathrooms – four each for men and women, segregated by the four primary racial groups, as mandated by law. Together, the eight bathrooms would consume one-quarter of an entire floor.

FitzGerald rejected the plans, announcing that he would build two bathrooms, one for men and one for women, to the highest possible standards. Once the plant was built, government officials inspected the building, noticed the discrepancy, and asked him what he planned to do about it. He responded, "They're not segregated because we chose not to do so. We don't agree with segregation. These are very fine toilets – you could have your lunch on the floor. I don't have a problem at all. You have a problem, and you have to decide what you are going to do. I'm doing nothing." The government did not respond immediately, but later the law was quietly changed. FitzGerald's act of rebellion was small, but it was consistent with his values and was the only stand he could have taken in good conscience. Living one's values in this way, in the face of opposition, is energizing. Bringing about change that can make a difference to the people around us gives meaning to our work, and for many people, it leads to a renewed commitment to their jobs.

For Rob, the manager who found himself reporting to an abusive boss, the first step was to look inward and admit that every day would be a challenge. By becoming very clear about his own core values, he could decide moment to moment how to deal with Martin's demands. He could determine whether a particular emotional reaction was a visceral response to a man he didn't respect or a reaction to a bad idea that he would need to confront. He could choose whether to do what he thought was right or to collude with what felt wrong. His clarity allowed him to stay calm and focused, do his job well, and take care of the business and the people around him. In the end, Rob came out of a difficult situation knowing he had kept his integrity without compromising his career, and in that time, he even learned and grew professionally. He still uses the barometer he developed during his years with Martin to check actions and decisions against his values, even though his circumstances have changed.

Another executive we've worked with, Bart Morrison, ran a nonprofit organization for ten years and was widely considered a success by donors, program recipients, and policy makers alike. Yet he felt restless and wondered if a turn as a company executive – which would mean higher compensation – would satisfy his urge for a new challenge. Morrison didn't really need more money, although it would have been a plus, and he had a deep sense of social mission and commitment to his work. He also acknowledged that working in the private sector would not realistically offer him any meaningful new challenges. In our work together, he brainstormed about different avenues he could take while continuing in the nonprofit field, and it occurred to him that he could write books and give speeches. These new activities gave him the excitement he had been looking for and allowed him to stay true to his calling.

It's worth noting that executives often feel threatened when employees start asking, "Am I doing what I want to do with my life?" The risk is very real that the answer will be no, and companies can lose great contributors. The impulse, then, may be to try to suppress such exploration. Many executives also avoid listening to their own signals, fearing that a close look at their dreams and aspirations will reveal severe disappointments, that to be true to themselves they will have to leave their jobs and sacrifice everything they have worked so hard to achieve.

But although people no longer expect leaders to have all the answers, they do expect their leaders to be open to the questions – to try to keep their own passion alive and to support employees through the same process. After all, sooner or later most people will feel an urgent need to take stock – and if they are given the chance to heed the call, they will most likely emerge stronger, wiser, and more determined than ever.

POSTSCRIPT

Originally Published on LinkedIn.com

ENTERING THE FLOW STATE

November 18, 2013

"Flow", the state where we feel in command of what we do, do it effortlessly, and perform at our best, was discovered by researchers at the University of Chicago. They asked a wide range of people, "Tell us about a time you outdid yourself – you performed at your peak." No matter who answered – ballerinas, chess champs, surgeons – they all described the flow state. One of flow's best features: it feels great.

Today we all realize that we do our best work in those special moments when we are in flow. And for leaders helping people get into flow and stay there means they will work at their peak abilities.

But how do you get into flow in the first place? I can think of three main pathways.

The first matches a person's tasks to his or her skill set. In the Chicago study, this was put in terms of the ratio of a person's abilities to the demand of the task. The more a challenge requires us to deploy our best skills, the more likely we will become absorbed in flow.

If we are under-challenged – it's too easy – our performance suffers and we end up bored or disengaged. That's the plight of a large portion of knowledge workers, some statistics suggest. Upping

the challenge would engage more of these people, and for a lucky few perhaps get them into flow.

Another path to flow lies in finding work we love. Doing what we're passionate about is one sign of "good work," the topic of research by Howard Gardner at Harvard, Bill Damon at Stanford, and Mihalyi Csikzentmihalyi, the discoverer of flow. In good work we align what we're best at doing with what engages us and also what fits our sense of meaning and purpose. Good work puts us in a frame of mind where, again, flow can arise spontaneously.

The final common pathway of any approach to flow is fully absorbed focus. The stronger the concentration we bring to a task, the more likely we are to drop into flow while doing it. While the other paths to flow depend on getting the externals right – the challenge/demand ratio, or finding work that aligns ethics, excellence and engagement – full focus is an inner dimension. The better our ability to pay attention to what we choose and ignore distractions, the stronger our concentration.

Strong focus can bring us into flow no matter the task at hand. This is an inner strength we develop and strengthen. Mindfulness, for instance, is one way to bulk up the muscle of attention, particularly if we use mindfulness to notice when we have wandered away from a chosen point of focus and bring our attention back. That, in fact, is the basic repetition for toning up concentration in the mental gym, according to research done at Emory University.

We can strengthen this ability on our own time, just as we would go to the gym after work. A daily mental workout where you use your breath as the point of concentration, and continually bring your wandering mind back to your breath, will bulk up your power to focus. Regular brain strengthening should help you find your way to flow no matter what you do.

SOCIAL INTELLIGENCE AND THE BIOLOGY OF LEADERSHIP

written with Richard Boyatzis

Originally published in the Harvard Business Review, September 2008

In 1998 I published my first article on emotional intelligence and leadership. The response to "What Makes a Leader?" was enthusiastic. People throughout and beyond the business community started talking about the vital role that empathy and self-knowledge play in effective leadership. The concept of emotional intelligence continues to occupy a prominent space in the leadership literature and in everyday coaching practices. But in the past five years, research in the emerging field of social neuroscience – the study of what happens in the brain while people interact – is beginning to reveal subtle new truths about what makes a good leader.

The salient discovery is that certain things leaders do – specifically, exhibit empathy and become attuned to others' moods – literally affect both their own brain chemistry and that of their followers. Indeed, researchers have found that the leader-follower dynamic is not a case of two (or more) independent brains reacting consciously or unconsciously to each other. Rather, the individual minds become, in a sense, fused into a single system. We believe that great leaders are those whose behavior powerfully leverages the system of brain interconnectedness. We place them on the opposite end of the neural continuum from people with serious social disorders, such as autism spectrum disorder, that are characterized by underdevelopment in the areas of the brain associated with social interactions. If we are correct, it follows that a potent way of becoming a better leader is to find authentic contexts in which to learn the kinds of social behavior that reinforce the brain's social circuitry. Leading effectively is, in other words, less about mastering situations – or even mastering social skill sets – than about developing a genuine interest in and talent for fostering positive feelings in the people whose cooperation and support you need.

The notion that effective leadership is about having powerful social circuits in the brain has prompted us to extend our concept of emotional intelligence, which we had grounded in theories of individual psychology. A more relationship-based construct for assessing leadership is social intelligence, which we define as a set of interpersonal competencies built on specific neural circuits (and related endocrine systems) that inspire others to be effective.

The idea that leaders need social skills is not new, of course. In 1920, Columbia University psychologist Edward Thorndike pointed out that "the best mechanic in a factory may fail as a foreman for lack of social intelligence." More recently, our colleague Claudio Fernández-Aráoz found in an analysis of new C-level executives that those who had been hired for their self-discipline, drive, and intellect were sometimes later fired for lacking basic social skills. In other words, the people Fernández-Aráoz studied had smarts in spades, but their inability to get along socially on the job was professionally self-defeating.

What's new about our definition of social intelligence is its biological underpinning, which we will explore in the following pages. Drawing on the work of neuroscientists, our own research and consulting endeavors, and the findings of researchers affiliated with the Consortium for Research on Emotional Intelligence in Organizations, we will show you how to translate newly acquired knowledge about mirror neurons, spindle cells, and oscillators into practical, socially intelligent behaviors that can reinforce the neural links between you and your followers.

FOLLOWERS MIRROR THEIR LEADERS: LITERALLY

Perhaps the most stunning recent discovery in behavioral neuroscience is the identification of mirror neurons in widely dispersed areas of the brain. Italian neuroscientists found them by accident while monitoring a particular cell in a monkey's brain that fired only when the monkey raised its arm. One day a lab assistant lifted an ice cream cone to his own mouth and triggered a reaction in the monkey's cell. It was the first evidence that the brain is peppered with neurons that mimic, or mirror, what another being does. This previously unknown class of brain cells operates as neural Wi-Fi, allowing us to navigate our social world. When we consciously or unconsciously detect someone else's emotions through their actions, our mirror neurons reproduce those emotions. Collectively, these neurons create an instant sense of shared experience.

Mirror neurons have particular importance in organizations, because leaders' emotions and actions prompt followers to mirror those feelings and deeds. The effects of activating neural circuitry in followers' brains can be very powerful. In a recent study, our colleague Marie Dasborough observed two groups: One received negative performance feedback accompanied by positive emotional signals – namely, nods and smiles; the other was given positive feedback that was delivered critically, with frowns and narrowed eyes. In subsequent interviews conducted to compare the emotional states of the two groups, the people who had received positive feedback accompanied by negative emotional signals reported feeling worse about their performance than did the participants who had received good-natured negative feedback. In effect, the delivery was more important than the message itself. And everybody knows that when people feel better, they perform better. So, if leaders hope to get the best out of their people, they should continue to be demanding but in ways that foster a positive mood in their teams. The old carrot-and-stick approach alone doesn't make neural sense; traditional incentive systems are simply not enough to get the best performance from followers.

Here's an example of what does work. It turns out that there's a subset of mirror neurons whose only job is to detect other people's smiles and laughter, prompting smiles and laughter in return. A boss who is self-controlled and humorless will rarely engage those neurons in his team members, but a boss who laughs and sets an easygoing tone puts those neurons to work, triggering spontaneous laughter and knitting his team together in the process. A bonded group is one that performs well, as our colleague Fabio Sala has shown in his research. He found that top-performing leaders elicited laughter from their subordinates three times as often, on average, as did mid-performing leaders. Being in a good mood, other research finds, helps people take in information effectively and respond nimbly and creatively. In other words, laughter is serious business.

It certainly made a difference at one university-based hospital in Boston. Two doctors we'll call Dr. Burke and Dr. Humboldt were in contention for the post of CEO of the corporation that ran this hospital and others. Both of them headed up departments, were superb physicians, and had published many widely cited research articles in prestigious medical journals. But the two had very different personalities. Burke was intense, task focused, and impersonal. He was a relentless perfectionist with a combative tone that kept his staff continually on edge. Humboldt was no less demanding, but he was very approachable, even playful, in relating to staff, colleagues, and patients. Observers noted that people smiled and teased one another – and even spoke their minds – more in Humboldt's department than in Burke's. Prized talent often ended up leaving Burke's department; in contrast, outstanding folks gravitated to Humboldt's warmer working climate. Recognizing Humboldt's socially intelligent leadership style, the hospital corporation's board picked him as the new CEO.

THE "FINELY ATTUNED" LEADER

Great executives often talk about leading from the gut. Indeed, having good instincts is widely recognized as an advantage for a leader in any context, whether in reading the mood of one's organization or in conducting a delicate negotiation with the competition. Leadership scholars characterize this talent as an ability to recognize patterns, usually born of extensive experience. Their advice: Trust your gut, but get lots of input as you make decisions. That's sound practice, of course, but managers don't always have the time to consult dozens of people.

Findings in neuroscience suggest that this approach is probably too cautious. Intuition, too, is in the brain, produced in part by a class of neurons called spindle cells because of their shape. They have a body size about four times that of other brain cells, with an extra-long branch to make attaching to other cells easier and transmitting thoughts and feelings to them quicker. This ultra-rapid connection of emotions, beliefs, and judgments creates what behavioral scientists call our social guidance system. Spindle cells trigger neural networks that come into play whenever we have to choose the best response among many – even for a task as routine as prioritizing a to-do list. These cells also help us gauge whether someone is trustworthy and right (or wrong) for a job. Within one-twentieth of a second, our spindle cells fire with information about how we feel about that person; such "thin-slice" judgments can be very accurate, as follow-up metrics reveal. Therefore, leaders should not fear to act on those judgments, provided that they are also attuned to others' moods.

Such attunement is literally physical. Followers of an effective leader experience rapport with her – or what we and our colleague Annie McKee call "resonance." Much of this feeling arises unconsciously, thanks to mirror neurons and spindle-cell circuitry. But another class of neurons is also involved: Oscillators coordinate people physically by regulating how and when their bodies move together. You can see oscillators in action when you watch people about to kiss; their movements look like a dance, one body responding to the other seamlessly. The same dynamic occurs when two cellists play together. Not only do they hit their notes in unison, but thanks to oscillators, the two musicians' right brain hemispheres are more closely coordinated than are the left and right sides of their individual brains.

FIRING UP YOUR SOCIAL NEURONS

The firing of social neurons is evident all around us. We once analyzed a video of Herb Kelleher, a cofounder and former CEO of Southwest Airlines, strolling down the corridors of Love Field in Dallas, the airline's hub. We could practically see him activate the mirror neurons, oscillators, and other social circuitry in each person he encountered. He offered beaming smiles, shook hands with customers as he told them how much he appreciated their business, hugged employees as he thanked them for their good work. And he got back exactly what he gave. Typical was the flight attendant whose face lit up when she unexpectedly encountered her boss. "Oh, my honey!" she blurted, brimming with warmth, and gave him a big hug. She later explained, "Everyone just feels like family with him."

Unfortunately, it's not easy to turn yourself into a Herb Kelleher or a Dr. Humboldt if you're not one already. We know of no clear-cut methods to strengthen mirror neurons, spindle cells, and oscillators; they activate by the thousands per second during any encounter, and their precise firing patterns remain elusive. What's more, self-conscious attempts to display social intelligence can often backfire. When you make an intentional effort to coordinate movements with another person, it is not only oscillators that fire. In such situations the brain uses other, less adept circuitry to initiate and guide movements; as a result, the interaction feels forced.

The only way to develop your social circuitry effectively is to undertake the hard work of changing your behavior. Companies interested in leadership development need to begin by assessing the willingness of individuals to enter a change program. Eager candidates should first develop a personal vision for change and then undergo a thorough diagnostic assessment, akin to a medical workup, to identify areas of social weakness and strength. Armed with the feedback, the aspiring leader can be trained in specific areas where developing better social skills will have the greatest payoff. The training can range from rehearsing better ways of interacting and trying them out at every opportunity, to being shadowed by a coach and then debriefed about what he observes, to learning directly from a role model. The options are many, but the road to success is always tough.

HOW TO BECOME SOCIALLY SMARTER

To see what social intelligence training involves, consider the case of a top executive we'll call Janice. She had been hired as a marketing manager by a Fortune 500 company because of her business expertise, outstanding track record as a strategic thinker and planner, reputation as a straight talker, and ability to anticipate business issues that were crucial for meeting goals. Within her first six months on the job, however, Janice was floundering; other executives saw her as aggressive and opinionated, lacking in political astuteness, and careless about what she said and to whom, especially higher-ups.

To save this promising leader, Janice's boss called in Kathleen Cavallo, an organizational psychologist and senior consultant with the Hay Group, who immediately put Janice through a 360-degree evaluation. Her direct reports, peers, and managers gave Janice low ratings on empathy, service orientation, adaptability, and managing conflicts. Cavallo learned more by having confidential conversations with the people who worked most closely with Janice. Their complaints focused on her failure to establish rapport with people or even notice their reactions. The bottom line: Janice was adept neither at reading the social norms of a group nor at recognizing people's emotional cues when she violated those norms. Even more dangerous, Janice did not realize she was being too blunt in managing upward. When she had a strong difference of opinion with a manager, she did not sense when to back off. Her "let's get it all on the table and mix it up" approach was threatening her job; top management was getting fed up.

When Cavallo presented this performance feedback as a wake-up call to Janice, she was of course shaken to discover that her job might be in danger. What upset her more, though, was the realization that she was not having her desired impact on other people. Cavallo initiated coaching sessions in which Janice would describe notable successes and failures from her day. The more time Janice spent reviewing these incidents, the better she became at recognizing the difference between expressing an idea with conviction and acting like a pit bull. She began to anticipate how people might react to her in a meeting or during a negative performance review. She rehearsed more-astute ways to present her opinions, and she developed a personal vision for change. Such mental preparation activates the social circuitry of the brain, strengthening the neural connections you need to act effectively; that's why Olympic athletes put hundreds of hours into mental review of their moves.

At one point, Cavallo asked Janice to name a leader in her organization who had excellent social intelligence skills. Janice identified a veteran senior manager who was masterly both in the art of the critique and at expressing disagreement in meetings without damaging relationships. She asked him to help coach her, and she switched to a job where she could work with him – a post she held for two years. Janice was lucky to find a mentor who believed that part of a leader's job is to develop human capital. Many bosses would rather manage around a problem employee than help her get better. Janice's new boss took her on because he recognized her other strengths as invaluable, and his gut told him that Janice could improve with guidance.

Before meetings, Janice's mentor coached her on how to express her viewpoint about contentious issues and how to talk to higher-ups, and he modeled for her the art of performance feedback. By observing him day in and day out, Janice learned to affirm people even as she challenged their positions or critiqued their performance. Spending time with a living, breathing model of effective behavior provides the perfect stimulation for our mirror neurons, which allow us to directly experience, internalize, and ultimately emulate what we observe.

DO WOMEN HAVE STRONGER SOCIAL CIRCUITS?

People often ask whether gender differences factor into the social intelligence skills needed for outstanding leadership. The answer is yes and no. It's true that women tend, on average, to be better than men at immediately sensing other people's emotions, whereas men tend to have more social confidence, at least in work settings. However, gender differences in social intelligence that are dramatic in the general population are all but absent among the most successful leaders.

When the University of Toledo's Margaret Hopkins studied several hundred executives from a major bank, she found gender differences in social intelligence in the overall group but not between the most effective men and the most effective women. Ruth Malloy of the Hay Group uncovered a similar pattern in her study of CEOs of international companies. Gender, clearly, is not neural destiny.

Janice's transformation was genuine and comprehensive. In a sense, she went in one person and came out another. If you think about it, that's an important lesson from neuroscience: Because our behavior creates and develops neural networks, we are not necessarily prisoners of our genes and our early childhood experiences. Leaders can change if, like Janice, they are ready to put in the effort. As she progressed in her training, the social behaviors she was learning became more like second nature to her. In scientific terms, Janice was strengthening her social circuits through practice. And as others responded to her, their brains connected with hers more profoundly and effectively, thereby reinforcing Janice's circuits in a virtuous circle. The upshot: Janice went from being on the verge of dismissal to getting promoted to a position two levels up.

A few years later, some members of Janice's staff left the company because they were not happy – so she asked Cavallo to come back. Cavallo discovered that although Janice had mastered the ability to communicate and connect with management and peers, she still sometimes missed cues from her direct reports when they tried to signal their frustration. With more help from Cavallo, Janice was able to turn the situation around by refocusing her attention on her staff's emotional needs and fine-tuning her communication style. Opinion surveys conducted with Janice's staff before and after Cavallo's second round of coaching documented dramatic increases in their emotional commitment and intention to stay in the organization. Janice and the staff also delivered a 6% increase in annual sales, and after another successful year she was made president of a multibillion-dollar unit. Companies can clearly benefit a lot from putting people through the kind of program Janice completed.

HARD METRICS OF SOCIAL INTELLIGENCE

Our research over the past decade has confirmed that there is a large performance gap between socially intelligent and socially unintelligent leaders. At a major national bank, for example, we found that levels of an executive's social intelligence competencies predicted yearly performance appraisals more powerfully than did the emotional intelligence competencies of self-awareness and self-management.

ARE YOU A SOCIALLY INTELLIGENT LEADER?

To measure an executive's social intelligence and help him or her develop a plan for improving it, we have a specialist administer our behavioral assessment tool, the Emotional and Social Competency Inventory. It is a 360-degree evaluation instrument by which bosses, peers, direct reports, clients, and sometimes even family members assess a leader according to seven social intelligence qualities.

We came up with these seven by integrating our existing emotional intelligence framework with data assembled by our colleagues at the Hay Group, who used hard metrics to capture the behavior of top-performing leaders at hundreds of corporations over two decades. Listed here are each of the qualities, followed by some of the questions we use to assess them.

Empathy

• Do you understand what motivates other people, even those from different backgrounds?

• Are you sensitive to others' needs?

Attunement

• Do you listen attentively and think about how others feel?

• Are you attuned to others' moods?

Organizational Awareness

• Do you appreciate the culture and values of the group or organization?

• Do you understand social networks and know their unspoken norms?

Influence

• Do you persuade others by engaging them in discussion and appealing to their self-interests?

• Do you get support from key people?

Developing Others

• Do you coach and mentor others with compassion and personally invest time and energy in mentoring?

• Do you provide feedback that people find helpful for their professional development?

Inspiration

• Do you articulate a compelling vision, build group pride, and foster a positive emotional tone?

• Do you lead by bringing out the best in people?

Teamwork

• Do you solicit input from everyone on the team?

• Do you support all team members and encourage cooperation?

Social intelligence turns out to be especially important in crisis situations. Consider the experience of workers at a large Canadian provincial health care system that had gone through drastic cutbacks and a reorganization. Internal surveys revealed that the frontline workers had become frustrated that they were no longer able to give their patients a high level of care. Notably, workers whose leaders scored low in social intelligence reported unmet patient-care needs at three times the rate – and emotional exhaustion at four times the rate – of their colleagues who had supportive leaders. At the same time, nurses with socially intelligent bosses reported good emotional health and an enhanced ability to care for their patients, even during the stress of layoffs. These results should be compulsory reading for the boards of companies in crisis. Such boards typically favor expertise over social intelligence when selecting someone to guide the institution through tough times. A crisis manager needs both.

As we explore the discoveries of neuroscience, we are struck by how closely the best psychological theories of development map to the newly charted hardwiring of the brain. Back in the 1950s, for example, British pediatrician and psychoanalyst D.W. Winnicott was advocating for play as a way to accelerate children's learning. Similarly, British physician and psychoanalyst John Bowlby emphasized the importance of providing a secure base from which people can strive toward goals, take risks without unwarranted fear, and freely explore new possibilities. Hard-bitten executives may consider it absurdly indulgent and financially untenable to concern themselves with such theories in a world where bottom-line performance is the yardstick of success. But as new ways of scientifically measuring human development start to bear out these theories and link them directly with performance, the so-called soft side of business begins to look not so soft after all.

THE CHEMISTRY OF STRESS

When people are under stress, surges in the stress hormones adrenaline and cortisol strongly affect their reasoning and cognition. At low levels, cortisol facilitates thinking and other mental functions, so well-timed pressure to perform and targeted critiques of subordinates certainly have their place. When a leader's demands become too great for a subordinate to handle, however, soaring cortisol levels and an added hard kick of adrenaline can paralyze the mind's critical abilities. Attention fixates on the threat from the boss rather than the work at hand; memory, planning, and creativity go out the window. People fall back on old habits, no matter how unsuitable those are for addressing new challenges.

Poorly delivered criticism and displays of anger by leaders are common triggers of hormonal surges. In fact, when laboratory scientists want to study the highest levels of stress hormones, they simulate a job interview in which an applicant receives intense face-to-face criticism – an analogue of a boss's tearing apart a subordinate's performance. Researchers likewise find that when someone who is very important to a person expresses contempt or disgust toward him, his stress circuitry triggers an explosion by stress hormones and a spike in heart rate of 30 to 40 beats per minute. Then, because of the interpersonal dynamic of mirror neurons and oscillators, the tension spreads to other people. Before you know it, the destructive emotions have infected an entire group and inhibited its performance.

Leaders are themselves not immune to the contagion of stress. All the more reason they should take the time to understand the biology of their emotions.

POSTSCRIPT

Originally Published on LinkedIn.com

THE KEY HABIT OF GOOD LEADERS

May 02, 2013

Leaders today are beset by overwhelming demands – scheduled every 15 minutes through the day, with an incoming barrage of messages via phone, email, texts, and knocks on the door. Who has time to pay full attention to the person you're with?

And yet it is in the moments of total attention that interpersonal chemistry occurs. This is when what we say has the most impact, when we can come up with the most fruitful ideas and collaborations, when negotiations and brainstorms are most productive.

And it all starts with listening, turning our attention fully to the person we are with. It's not just leaders, of course. We're all besieged by distractions, falling behind on our to-do lists, multi-tasking.

A classic study of doctors and patients asked people in the physician's waiting room how many questions they had for their doctor. The average was around four. The number of questions they actually asked during that visit with their doctor turned out to be about one-and-a-half. The reason? Once the patient started talking, an average of 16 seconds or so the doctor would cut them off and take over the conversation.

That's a good analog for what happens in offices everywhere. We're too busy (we think) to take the time to listen fully.

This leads to the common cold of the workplace: Tuning out of what that person is saying before we fully understand – and telling them what we think too soon. Real listening means hearing the person out and then responding, in a mutual dialogue.

So there you have a bad habit to replace – poor listening – and a positive alternative to practice instead.

People are notoriously poor at changing habits. Neuroscience findings make clear why: habits operate from the basal ganglia, in the unconscious part of the mind. They are automatic and most often invisible, even as they drive what we do.

This arrangement works well, for the most part. The basal ganglia's repertoire of unconscious habits includes everything from how to operate your smartphone (once you've mastered the details) to how to brush your teeth. We don't want to have to think about these routines – and our brain doesn't want to waste on them the mental energy that would take.

But when it comes to our unhelpful habits, that arrangement creates a barrier to changing them for the better. We don't notice them, and so have no control. We need to become consciously aware of the habit, which transfers control to the brain's executive centers in the prefrontal area. This offers us a choice we did not have before.

The key is being mindful of those moments in your day when you have a naturally occurring opportunity to practice good listening. Most often those moments go by unnoticed and we launch into our old, bad habits.

Once you notice the moment is here, there's another task for mindfulness: to remind you of the better habit. In this case, you would intentionally put aside what you're doing, ignore your phone and email, stop your own train of thought – and pay full attention to the person in front of you.

AN ANTIDOTE TO THE DARK SIDE OF EI

January 05, 2014

Let's not idealize emotional intelligence. Like any other human skill set – IQ, hacking skills, strength – it can be used for self-serving ends or for the common good, as addressed in

Adam Grant's article for The Atlantic titled The Dark Side of Emotional Intelligence.

You see the dark side at work when EI gets used to manipulate others, not for the betterment of an organization. Emotional intelligence (or EI), in my model, refers to our ability to read and understand emotions in ourselves and others, and to handle those feelings effectively. In general, a high level of EI predicts better success in school and in career, in relationships and in leading a fulfilled life. For leaders EI can make the difference between success and failure.

But EI is not just one single ability that we are good at or not – we can have strengths in one part of EI – like excellent self-management, the key to self-discipline, achieving goals, and "grit" – while lacking in other parts, like empathy or social skills. In fact that very pattern is common in the workplace, marking those who are outstanding individual performers (at programming, say) but who are not able to work well as part of a team or as a leader.

Within each component of EI we can make nuanced distinctions. So when it comes to empathy – the ability to understand how another person experiences the world – there are different types, each with its own benefits.

Cognitive empathy refers to being able to sense how another person thinks. It can help us be better communicators by putting things in terms the other person understands. Research shows that managers with this kind of empathy get better-than-expected results from their direct reports. And executives with high cognitive empathy do better at overseas assignments because they can more quickly pick up the implicit social norms and mental models of a new culture.

Emotional empathy means we feel in ourselves the other person's emotions – our feelings resonate. People adept at emotional empathy can form warm bonds with others, and have good chemistry. Such rapport makes negotiations, teamwork and just about any shared task go better.

Then there's empathic concern, sensitivity to other people's needs and the readiness to help if need be. Workers with such concern are the good citizens of any organization, the ones everyone else knows can be counted on to help when the pressure is on. Among leaders, those with empathic concern create a "secure base," the sense that your boss has your back, will support and protect you as needed, and gives you the security to take risks and try new ways of operating – the key to innovation.

This is the kind of empathy that serves as an antidote to the dark side of emotional intelligence – the manipulative use of talents in EI in the service of one's own interest, and at the expense of others. Narcissists,

Machiavellians and sociopaths all do this, as I've detailed in *Focus: The Hidden Driver of Excellence*. A Norwegian study found that men who lacked empathic concern in childhood were far more likely than others as adults to end up as felons in prison.

Empathic concern means we care about the well-being of the people around us. It's the opposite motivation of the self-serving types who use whatever influence or other empathy abilities solely in their own interests – the Bernie Madoffs among us. Empathic concern is what to look for when hiring, when promoting, and when developing leadership talent.

THE LEADER'S TRIPLE FOCUS

Adapted from *Focus: The Hidden Driver of Excellence*

A primary task of leadership is to direct attention. Leaders tell us where to focus our energies. But leaders need, too, to manage their own attention. Leaders who do this effectively can soar, those who do not will stumble. The reason is simple. "Your focus," Yoda reminds us, "is your reality."

To direct attention well requires a keen grasp of where, when, why, and toward what we need to aim our awareness. Leaders do this in many ways. Simply articulating a new strategy, for instance, signals a shift in organizational attention. People in each core function, from finance to marketing, will make that shift in their own way.

Why my focus on focus itself? I grounded my writing about emotional intelligence in two then-new disciplines, affective and social neuroscience. Affective neuroscience pulled back the curtain on how our brains manage emotion; social neuroscience revealed the power of a virtual brain-to-brain linkage that acts as a conduit for emotions during our interactions. Both together have offered telling insights for understanding the power of emotional intelligence in leadership.

140

More recently I've been tracking a boom in findings on the brain and attention, as scientists have imaged the brain activity of people engaged in the varieties of focusing. This new science has led me to a keen appreciation of the subtle, yet powerful, role of attention in the art of leadership.

For one, the neuroanatomy of attention and emotion show them to be surprisingly interwoven in the brain's circuitry. Emotions are the brain's way of directing attention; managing attention is the mind's way of controlling emotion.

A slight shift in our lens on emotional intelligence highlights how focus matters for leadership. The emotional intelligence competencies that set the best leaders apart from average, it turns out, are interwoven with elements of attention, even at the most basic level of neural wiring.

Self-awareness and self-management, empathy and relationship management, are the four main components of emotional intelligence. Self-awareness and its resulting abilities in self-management depend on our shifting attention inward. Empathy, the foundation of handling relationships well, requires a keen attention to others.

To this inner and other-directed focus for leaders, I would add a third orientation: an outer awareness that can read the meaningful current within an organization and scan for events and forces that impact it. Every leader needs a triad of awareness – Inner, Other, and Outer – in abundance, in proper balance, and with the flexibility to exercise the right one at the right time. Too little of any one of these can make a leader vulnerable to being rudderless, clueless, or blindsided – or, worse, all three.

INNER FOCUS

Leaders today are besieged by distractions: urgent messages, appointments every fifteen minutes, decisions ranging from people to strategy. A decade or two ago few executives traveled with the technology that means wherever they go they are aswim in a running stream of messages and data, 24/7. Now most all do.

That flow of intrusions draw attention away from what's immediately at hand; those seemingly urgent ring tones may not be for what's important right now. The struggle to maintain sharp focus on what matters despite intrusions rages within the brain's circuitry for attention.

"Cognitive effort" is the scientific term for the mental work demanded by our daily information load. Like our muscles, our attention can be overworked. Attention fatigue shows up as lowered effectiveness with increased distractedness and irritability. These signal depletion in the glucose that feeds neural energy.

Concentration means selecting a single point of focus and resisting the pull of everything else – sifting through to find what's important in the sea of irrelevancies. Executives who do this well are able to monitor their own attention; they are energized and concentrated rather than flagging and distracted.

But a concentrated focus on goals is not the only kind of attention leaders need. Creativity and innovation, for instance, demand a more open and relaxed attention. Here again self-awareness shows its value: monitoring ourselves lets us check whether our mode of attention suits the need of the moment.

In "top-down" attention we actively choose what we attend to. "Bottom up" attention means we are living on automatic, letting our focus be dictated by whatever comes along; this can make us unwitting puppets of the preferences and blindspots of our unconscious mind. There is a place for this in life, of course – just not necessarily at work.

"Cognitive control" is the scientific term for paying attention where we want and keeping it there in the face of temptations to wander – an essential mental ability in self-awareness. This concentrated focus represents one aspect of the brain's executive function, located in the prefrontal cortex – the area just behind the forehead that acts as the brain's manager.

Consider the implications for leadership of a gold standard study of life success, a longitudinal project in Dunedin, New Zealand, that rigorously tested more than one thousand boys and girls on their cognitive control, and then tracked them down again when they had reached their 30s. The stunning result: their childhood ability to focus on one thing and ignore distractions was a stronger predictor of their adult financial success than either their IQ or the wealth of the family they grew up in.

In executives, cognitive control holds the key to leadership competencies like self-management – the ability to focus on a goal and the discipline to pursue it despite distractions and setbacks. The same neural circuitry that allows such one-pointed pursuit of goals also manages unruly emotions. Good cognitive control can be seen in those executives who stay calm in crisis, tame their own agitation, and recover from debacle or defeat.

Self-awareness can be seen, too, in those executives who are clear and candid about their strengths and their limits. While this means they can be confident in their performance when they are working from those strengths, it also means they know when their limitations mean to rely on someone else who has strong abilities in that area.

Another variety of self-awareness attunes us to internal neural circuitry that monitors our entire body, including our internalized ethical algorithms for what feels right and what wrong. These primal brain circuits send their messages to us via the body, particularly the gut. USC neuroscientist Antonio Damasio calls these gut feelings "somatic markers," an inner rudder that tells us for any decision the sum total of relevant lessons learned from our lifetime's experience.

Our gut sense of what to do – and what not to do – gives us direction in keeping with our values. When a young film-maker saw how the studio he worked for edited his first major film he was deeply upset that he had lost creative control. So he took the money he made from that film and went off on his own to make a second one, despite the advice of all his friends in the business that he let a studio risk their money on it – not put his own dollars on the line. But he felt the artistic integrity of his film was more important.

When he had almost completed the film his money ran out. Bank after bank turned him down for a loan. The tenth bank he approached finally gave him the last financing he needed. That last-minute loan let George Lucas finish Star Wars.

Of course following your heart is no guarantee of a business empire like LucasFilm. But it does up the odds of finding what researchers call "good work," which combines our values, what we are best at, and what we love doing. Leaders who find this rare mix of ethics, excellence and exhilaration in their work will guide with a contagion of energy and enthusiasm.

OTHER FOCUS

Other awareness shows itself in those who can readily find common ground and rapport with a new business associate, or get people to laugh and smile – not at a joke, but because of their sense of ease in the relationship. Their keen Other awareness lets them know in a presentation, for instance, when a listener needs a switch from cold data to a telling anecdote – or the other way around. These are the executives who people seek to work with, and whose opinions carry most weight.

You can recognize a heightened Other awareness in those executives who are quick to read the pulse of a group, recognizing an unspoken consensus. They will be the one to say, "So we've agreed that…" as everyone nods.

Strengths here also allow people to emerge as natural leaders in groups, even when they are not designated as such. You can spot such emergent leaders not by asking people to name the group's leader but rather by asking, "Who is the most influential person on the team?"

There are three kinds of empathy, each essential for leadership effectiveness. Cognitive empathy lets a leader understand another person's perspective, the mental models through which he sees his world. This lets a leader couch a message in the terms that will make most sense to that person, and so be more persuasive. Leaders with strengths here get better than expected performance from their direct reports.

Emotional empathy, in contrast, allows a leader to sense immediately how someone feels at that moment. This ability lets a leader have interactions high in chemistry, the feeling of resonance that builds a sense of connection, trust and understanding. Everything goes more smoothly in such near-magic moments, whether a shared business decision or a negotiation. Executives with strength in this variety of empathy can excel as mentors, client managers and group leaders, sensing in the moment how someone is reacting.

The third, empathic concern, means a leader senses the needs of those around him. This lets her spontaneously respond to what people feel matters most to them. The best organizational citizens show this kind of empathy when they voluntarily help someone else out. In leaders it can show up in creating an atmosphere of security, trust and support, where direct reports feel safe enough to take risks and explore new possibilities. When your leader has your back, you can act with more confidence.

And, in general, empathy of any kind makes people good listeners who build strong interpersonal connections, and who move through the organization

146

making positive impacts. They naturally build links and personal networks that let them guide and influence, motivate and communicate with power.

OUTER FOCUS

The dynamics of any organization can be seen as a system. At a global tech firm, for example, the shouting matches between the COO and his CEO ramified at every level down the organization, with rivalries and jealousies rampant. Collaboration was seen as a dangerous risk. The organization hemorrhaged talent.

The consultant brought in to deal with this management crisis recognized a dynamic he had seen earlier in his career, when he did systems-based family therapy: conflict between marital partners replicates in troubled relationships among their children. While therapy can potentially heal these rifts, sometimes a divorce becomes the only alternative. So, too, with the company. The troubled dynamic down-shifted when the CEO moved on to a second career.

"Getting the system into the room" refers to the practice of gathering all stakeholders of a given problem – the sometimes wide range of people who each hold degrees of control over systems that interplay. WalMart used this systems method to solve the problem posed by its magazines, 65% of which languished on store shelves and then were pulped – a waste of money and source of needless carbon emissions.

One of the big problems: magazines charged their advertisers by how many pages they bought rather than by how many were actually sold – their inducement was simply to get the magazines on to the shelves. By convening publishers and distributors to look at the entire system, WalMart was able to both better match particular magazines to the stores where they sold the most and get publishers to change how they charged for their ads. The result: a 50% reduction in wasted magazines.

Being able to read the larger systems that create and roil a company's ecological niche lets a leader formulate better strategies. This systems view played an explicit role, for instance, in the business strategies formulated by Whole Foods Market co-CEO John Mackey, which try to create benefits for a wide range of stakeholders, from customers, employees and stockholders to communities and the environment.

There are many signs that an executive has a sharp outer focus. These are people whose wide-ranging curiosity drives an unusually inclusive daily information scan, checking not just standard news sites and those pertaining to their business, but reaching out to unusual sources. They are open to the many surprising ways seemingly unrelated data can inform their central interests.

And they are constant learners, taking a genuine interest in new understanding they can get from other people. Their need to know turns any human encounter – whether with the person next to them on a plane, a factory foreman, or a chance visitor – an opportunity to learn about the other person's world. This sense of genuine interest makes them not just good listeners, but good questioners.

An outer awareness also reveals itself in a knack for detecting meaningful patterns in a spreadsheet, a fog of data, or the week's headlines. This talent makes an executive an adept curator of a sea of big data, able to pick out what counts and explain its significance. This knack for reading systems can be seen, too, in the ability to sense the farflung consequences of a local decision, or how a choice made today might matter into the far future.

IN THE MIND'S GYM

Reflect for a moment on attention and how you use it. The answer for most of us is likely to be, not as well as I might.

Attention is a mental muscle; like any other muscle, it can be strengthened through the right kind of exercise. The fundamental "rep" in building attention can be seen when your mind wanders, you notice it has wandered, and you bring it back to your desired point of focus and keep it there.

That basic movement in attention is at the root of virtually every kind of meditation, from mindfulness to the transcendental sort. Peeling away the layers of belief and cosmology that have been wrapped around meditation for centuries, cognitive scientists view it as simply the retraining of our habits of attention. And just as working out in a gym has carryover benefits for fitness in the rest of life, the attention-building that goes on during a meditation session generalizes to other mental tasks.

For decades research has shown that people who meditate are more concentrated in whatever else they do. The most recent findings from brain imaging show why: meditation strengthens the circuitry in the prefrontal cortex that guides attention.

There are two main kinds of attention focus, one-pointedness – bringing attention back to one point whenever it wanders away – and mindfulness, cultivating a witnessing awareness of whatever enters the mind.

Practicing one-pointed focus builds concentration, calmness and quicker recovery from the agitation of stress. Mindfulness adds to these a keen self-awareness. Because leaders need all these capacities in spades, companies from General Mills to Google have offered mindfulness training to their executives.

Google's program, "Search Inside Yourself," is now being deployed in other companies. A Stanford study of its effects found participants better at self-awareness – observing their own experience and acting with awareness – and better able to use the muscle of attention deployment to manage their own emotions, a key skill in the heat of the moment when focus gets hijacked. Also improved: empathic concern and listening skills.

FLEXIBILITY AND BALANCE

Inner, Other and Outer focus are synergistic. A keen Outer focus, for instance, helps a leader grasp the right strategic vision. But she can only put that into action by communicating and mobilizing her people. That might take, for instance, articulating a shared vision she genuinely believes in, and doing so in a way that people resonate with: from the heart to the heart.

Each of these three kinds of focus and their sub-varieties has its benefits, and leaders need all three in balance: the right one for the right purpose at the right time. Being weak in any of them has drawbacks.

Take the varieties of Outer focus deployed in strategy. Many businesses succeed by executing a specific range of jobs well; strategic thinkers call this operational focus "exploitation." Jack Welch's insistence when he was CEO of GE that the corporation drop businesses that were not first or second in their sector exemplifies exploitation.

Other firms find success through continual innovation and creative breakthroughs; this high-risk, high-reward approach is called "exploration." Exploration is the entrepreneur's strategy, searching for the next new thing. Think Steve Jobs at Apple. Of course Apple also exploited its winning technologies, and GE continued to innovate – any robust company needs to do both.

Exploitation requires concentration and continually returning attention to the job at hand. Exploration demands an open focus, one that scans widely and recognizes new possibilities. Recent brain studies show that these two attention styles each operate in different circuits of the brain. Executives who grow too accustomed to one or the other, failing to exercise both, may find it hard to switch as needed – and the companies they lead may fail to balance exploitation with exploration.

Intel's founding CEO, Andrew Grove, dubs the tendency of companies to exploit a successful product or strategy for too long a "success trap." Any strategy, no matter how profitable at the moment, will have to change dramatically at some point if a company is to thrive into the long future.

RIM, for instance, stuck to exploitation of its Blackberry along with a disastrous lack of exploration as its market niche evolved. The founding co-CEOs, both engineers, had conquered their market via superior engineering, and stuck to that strategy. But as RIM lost a huge amount of market share, a new CEO was brought in. In his analysis holding to the exploitation strategy had left the company far behind its competitors in smartphone innovations like the faster 4G wireless network and touchscreens.

Simon Baron-Cohen, an Oxford University psychologist, describes two "brain styles," found in a portion of people at the extremes of a bell curve. At one extreme, a high level of systems awareness goes hand-in-hand with a deficit in empathy. In the opposite extreme people with high empathy suffer systems blindness. Neither style makes for the most effective leadership, though each shows up in various guises in executive ranks. Ideally a leader can both connect with people and read the meaningful signals amidst the systems noise.

There are other leadership maladies from being out-of-focus. An achievement-driven leader, for instance, fixates on hitting the numbers at the cost of connection to people. That leadership style has become more common in the higher ranks of firms since the onset of the fiscal crisis. Getting applause for those numbers can lead to a leader tuning out the negative interpersonal toll of his style. Such leaders have a myopic Other focus, seeing spending time with people as an interruption rather than a chance to connect, motivate, listen, and guide.

But consider the opposite imbalance. The charismatic and popular head of an Asian division of a global manufacturing company knew that he should be spending more time thinking about strategy. But he found his heart was not in it; what he loved doing was mixing with his workers on the shop floor, where he had begun his own career. His Other focus was out of proportion. An executive coach's intervention helped him get his attention priorities right, amping up his Outer focus.

THE FUTURE OF FOCUS

There are clear signs that the very ability to focus has come under siege today. Anyone who knows a teenager can vouch for young Millenials' addiction to their tech, like texting (which has leapt ahead of phone calls as their preferred mode for keeping in touch). In the new social ground rule, ignoring the people you are with by locking into an electronic device has become the norm, not rudeness.

Teachers tell me that many high school and college students today routinely keep a laptop on their desk during lectures – ostensibly to take notes, but actually to game, email, scroll through Facebook and like digital pursuits. At the same time teachers say more students have a harder time than those in the past sustaining their focus on a complex narrative. This may foretell a future generation of workers who have trouble understanding intricate ideas and paying attention for prolonged periods – already the conventional wisdom in media circles is "keep it short."

The neural circuitry for attention continues to take shape throughout childhood and adolescence. Sustained periods of full concentration strengthen this circuitry. Chronic distractedness undermines cognitive control. Threatened, too, are the inner awareness that allows for effective self-management in life, and the empathy that lets us attune to other people and coordinate what we do.

The emotional intelligence skill set, so vital for success in any field and essential for leadership, begins in the thick of life. We learn from our parents, family, friends, teachers, co-workers – if we pay attention to them. Any interaction can yield one lesson or another in this set of life skills, if only adding to our ability for empathy. The more time our young spend isolating themselves, staring at a digital screen, the less opportunity they will have for such learning.

My fear is that as these generations take their place in organizations and should – in theory – be in line for leadership positions, they may lack the fundamental basis in focus and emotional intelligence they will need. This means that organizations may have to embark on remedial programs in the focusing abilities that undergird people skills.

One emerging solution uses the love of gaming among the young to teach attention skills. At the University of Wisconsin, for instance, cognitive neuroscientists have teamed with digital designers to develop a game where sustained calm and concentration are the winning strategies.

Another approach teaches young children the basics of concentration in a daily five or ten-minute group activity where they simply observe the rise and fall of their belly as they breathe. Simple, to be sure – but that daily mental workout seems to strengthen the circuits for cognitive control that make young brains ready for learning (it works for adults, too). I've seen classrooms in inner city schools where this pays off with the focused atmosphere where students learn best.

Many schools today include programs in "social/emotional learning," which teach the basics of emotional intelligence like self-awareness and empathy, integrated with the standard school curriculum from kindergarten through high school. One meta-analysis of studies including a total of more than 270,000 students showed the programs led to substantial drops in anti-social behavior, hikes in cooperation and liking school – and an 11 percent boost in academic achievement scores.

Such youngsters include our leaders of the future. If community schools teach them the focusing skills they will need for their lives and careers, then companies will need to do less remedial focus-building as they become employees. Think of it as leadership training.

POSTSCRIPT

Originally Published on hbr.com
and LinkedIn.com

TO STRENGTHEN YOUR ATTENTION SPAN, STOP OVERTAXING IT

hbr.com - November 28, 2013

The Iditarod dog sled race covers 1,100 miles of Arctic ice and takes more than a week. The standard strategy for mushers had been to run twelve hours at a stretch, then rest for twelve. Either you ran all day and rested at night, or you rested all day and ran all night.

That all changed because of Susan Butcher, a veterinarian's assistant keenly aware of the biological limits of her dogs. She trained them to run in four-to-six hour spurts, and then rest for the same length of time, racing at that rhythm both night and day. She and her dogs won the race four times.

Susan Butcher trained her dogs the same way top athletes train in most any sport: an intense workout for about four hours – and then rest. That's the best routine for the body to attain maximal performance.

Anders Ericcson, a psychologist at the University of Florida who studies top performers, has found that world-class competitors from weight lifters to pianists limit the arduous part of their practice routine to a maximum of about four hours each day. Rest is part of their training regimen, to restore their physical and mental energy. They push themselves to their max, but not past it.

This work-rest-work-rest cycle also applies to helping our brain maintain maximal focus at work. In the workplace, concentrated focus allows us to use our skills at their peak. Researchers at the University of Chicago found, for instance, that at moments when people perform at the top of their game they are completely absorbed in the task at hand, whether brain surgery or making a three-pointer in basketball.

Top performance requires full focus, and sustaining focused attention consumes energy – more technically, your brain exhausts its fuel, glucose. Without rest, our brains grow more depleted. The signs of a brain running on empty include, for instance, distractedness, irritability, fatigue, and finding yourself checking Facebook when you should be doing your work.

A reasonable response is one executives today rarely make: give yourself a break. All too often we try to "push through it." But there is no magical energy reserve waiting for us – our performance will more likely slowly deteriorate as we push on through the day.

The decay in cognitive efficiency as we push past our reserves – well-documented in research labs – shows up in an executive's day as a mounting level of mistakes, forgetting, and momentary blankouts. As one executive put it, "When I notice that my mind has been somewhere else during a meeting, I wonder what opportunities I've been missing right here."

Given the high expectations on executives, perhaps it's understandable some have turned to performance-enhancing drugs. One lawyer who daily takes a medication for attention deficit disorder (which he does not have) confided to his physician, "If I didn't take this, I couldn't read contracts."

But there are other ways – legal and healthy – to help beef up our attention to meet the relentless demands of an executive's busy day: meditation. From the perspective of cognitive science all meditation methods are methods to train attention. An increasingly popular method to grow the power of the brain's circuitry for attention is "mindfulness," a meditation method stripped of a religious belief system.

The neuroscience behind mindfulness hinges on the concept of "neuroplasticity." The brain changes with repeated experience as some circuits strengthen and others wither.

Attention is a mental muscle, and can be strengthened with the right practice. The basic move to enhance concentration in the mental gym: put your focus on a chosen target, like your breath. When it wanders away (and it will), notice that your mind has wandered. This requires mindfulness, the ability to observe our thoughts without getting caught up in them.

Then bring your attention back to your breath. That's the mental equivalent of a weightlifting rep. Researchers at Emory University report that this simple exercise actually strengthens connectivity in the circuits for focus.

There's also another option. Call it the Latin Solution.

I was in Barcelona recently, where at lunchtime most shops and companies shutter themselves so employees can go home, have a good meal – and, ideally, take a nap. Even a short rest at mid-day reboots the brain for the rest of the day.

THREE QUICK FIXES FOR THE WANDERING MIND

linkedin.com - September 25, 2013

It happens to all of us: you're working away

on something you've got to get done, and suddenly you realize that for quite some time you've been lost in a reverie about something else entirely. You don't know when your mind went off track, nor how long you've been meandering down this one.

Our minds wander, on average 50 percent of the time. The exact rate varies enormously. When Harvard researchers had 2,250 people report what they were doing and what they were thinking about at random points throughout their day, the doing-thinking gaps ranged widely.

But the biggest gap was during work: mind-wandering is epidemic on the job. But we can take steps that will help us stay on task more of the time when we need to.

1. **Manage your temptations**. Many of the distractors that pull us away from what we're working on are digital: tweets, emails, and the like. There are several apps that can wall off those temptations to wander off. Chrome has two free apps that do this: Nanny for Google blocks off websites you might be tempted to visit, for whatever length of time you decide; StayFocusd limits the amount of time (also set by you) you can spend in your inbox, on Facebook, or wherever else you might be seduced away.

2. **Monitor your mind and take second thoughts**. Noticing where your mind has gone – checking your Twitter feed instead of working on that report – gives you the chance for a second thought: "my mind has wandered off again." That very thought disengages your brain from where it has wandered and activates brain circuits that can help your attention get unstuck and return to the work at hand.

3. **Practice a daily mindfulness session**. This mental exercise can be as simple as watching your breath, noticing when your mind has wandered off, letting go of the wandering thought and bringing it back to your breath again. These movements of the mind are like a mental workout, the equivalent of repetitions in lifting free weights: every rep strengthens the muscle a bit more. In mindfulness what gets stronger are the brain's circuits for noticing when your mind has wandered, letting go, and returning to your chosen focus. And that's just what we need to stay with during that one important task we're working on.

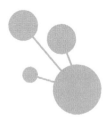

NOT JUST SMART BUT WISE

WHY GREAT LEADERS NEED TO HAVE A FOCUS BEYOND THEIR ORGANIZATIONS

Originally published in Egon Zehnder's *The Focus* Magazine, December 2013

I remember the exact moment when Paul Polman entered the pantheon of leaders I admire greatly. We were on a panel together at the Davos World Economic Forum, and Paul, CEO of Unilever, was describing his company's sustainability strategy. It wasn't the company's target to shrink the organization's carbon footprint that hooked me – as laudable as those goals are, these are common ingredients of corporate sustainability strategies. But Paul went on to announce that his company would strive to source raw materials in a new network of 500,000 smallholder farmers throughout the Third World. That was what got me.

Around 85 percent of farms worldwide are classed as smallholders. The World Bank names supporting smallholder farming as the single most effective way to stimulate economic development in rural areas. In emerging markets, agriculture supports – directly or indirectly – three out of four of those in the lowest income brackets.

Redrawing Unilever's supply chain in this way would leave more money in local farming communities, while boosting their children's health and education. In his thinking, the company's CEO had gone way beyond the normal boundaries of creating value for his own organization. Paul Polman's strategic vision exemplifies what I call an Outer focus, one of three kinds of focus every leader needs today: Outer, Other, and Inner.

EMOTIONAL INTELLIGENCE COMPETENCIES

Inner and Other focus can be seen in terms of emotional intelligence competencies. The first two of four emotional intelligence domains – self-awareness and self-management – signify a healthy Inner focus. They manifest among outstanding leaders in self-awareness strengths like a realistic self-confidence and an awareness of one's own strengths and limitations. Self-management reveals itself in emotional self-control (like staying calm and clear under high stress or recovering from it quickly), in adaptability, and in staying undistracted in pursuing goals.

In addition, a well-honed self-awareness helps a leader attune to the subtle internal signals that are the brain's way of letting the mind know what our life wisdom says about a decision we are pondering. This mechanism seems to be the avenue by which we sense in the first instant where our guiding values point us. Integrity and a sense of ethics depend on this inner prodding: Only after we get this felt sense can we put our values into words.

A robust Other focus, in the emotional intelligence model, shows up in leaders as an astute empathy, sensing how others think about the world – and so putting things in terms they understand – and resonating with how others feel in the moment. From this clear sense of others come relationship competencies like teamwork and collaboration, persuasion and influence, handling conflicts, and mentoring.

These "people skills" matter for leadership effectiveness over and above purely cognitive abilities like crunching numbers. Claudio Fernández-Aráoz, Senior Adviser at Egon Zehnder International, analyzed cases where seemingly outstanding hires for C-level positions ended up being let go. His conclusion: they were hired for their business expertise and intelligence, but fired for lapses in emotional intelligence.

STRENGTHS OF A THIRD KIND

But in addition to Inner and Other focus, I believe leaders today need strengths in a third kind of focus: Outer. An Outer focus allows a leader to sense the workings of the larger systems that shape an organization's fate – or a community's or society's. This goes beyond sensing coming changes in the winds of the economy, to include, for instance, social, cultural, and environmental forces at play.

When it comes to identifying emerging leaders, even while they are still in school, these three varieties of focus offer clues. Research finds that many of the abilities that mark outstanding leaders begin to emerge early in life, long before they enter the world of work. An astute inner awareness might reveal itself, for instance, in teenagers drawn to doing volunteer work for a cause larger than their own personal concerns, like the environment.

Another manifestation might be in superior self-management in the form of a single-minded focus on goals; researchers call this mental capacity "cognitive control." Many studies have found that cognitive control, when measured in children, predicts their financial success and health in adulthood more strongly than either their IQ or the wealth of their family of origin.

SKILLFUL MEANS

A well-honed Other awareness takes the form of heightened empathy, the ability to sense how others think and feel. Tuning in to the inner world of other people creates a platform for concern about their problems and pains – in other words, compassion. That social awareness also manifests as the interpersonal adeptness seen in high-performing leaders (or teachers, for that matter) who can connect quickly person-to-person, listen deeply, and influence others for the better. When empathy and social adeptness combine in the service of compassion, it becomes what Tibetans call 'skillful means,' effectiveness that does good.

And a precocious Outer focus might emerge in children and teens who are fascinated by natural systems, trying on their own initiative (rather than as a school assignment) to understand the workings of nature. This can also show up as a fascination with the 'STEM' topics: science, technology, engineering, and mathematics. Youngsters who love learning how things work are expressing a natural openness to systems thinking.

Yet when it comes to an Outer focus – which allows us to monitor the larger systems that shape our organizations, lives, society, and planet – we touch on a domain where the wisdom of one generation needs to be passed on to the next. This has become particularly true in transmitting critical knowledge for our species' survival.

That transmission has broken down in some crucial ways; while native cultures have always been keenly attuned to the workings of their local ecosystem in order to survive, in modern life we can stumble through, oblivious to the ways in which our local decisions can harm not just nearby, but also distant or invisible ecologies.

THE ANTHROPOCENE DILEMMA

Perhaps the gravest systemic crisis of our day goes largely unnoticed: the Anthropocene dilemma. We entered the Anthropocene age with the Industrial Revolution. Since then human systems for transportation, energy, construction, industry, and commerce have been steadily decaying the handful of global systems that support life on our planet.

While carbon's role in climate change has been the most visible of these systemic impacts, a huge array of others, from phosphorous-based fertilizer runoff creating dead spots in the world's water, to the buildup in human tissues of toxins like endocrine disrupters and carcinogens are largely unheralded.

Corporate leaders who demand more transparency about such impacts in their own operations and throughout their supply chain, and who make decisions that lessen their footprints, display outstanding systems awareness. Their Outer focus lets them operate in ways that go beyond the logic of economics alone, and to bring a more complex calculus into play that balances financial return with public welfare.

The leadership world has paid much attention to cultivating and identifying the abilities that allow an executive to navigate an organization through formulating smart strategies, to execute strategic goals and to grapple with the problems of the day. But we need more leaders with a wider vision, ones who do not settle for conditions as they are, but rather see what they could become, and work to change them.

TO TARGET THE GREATER GOOD

Our times demand leaders who are not just smart, but wise. Wise leaders formulate strategies that target the greater good, not just one organization's aims. The more our communities, societies and the world at large choose such leaders, the better off we will be. And the more skilled we become at spotting the potential for such leadership in younger generations – and helping them cultivate those qualities – the more hopeful our future.

I'm inspired by the words of Larry Brilliant, President of the Skoll Global Threats Fund, which seeks to prevent worldwide crises like pandemics and global warming. He says: "Civilizations should be judged not by how they treat people closest to power, but rather how they treat those furthest from power – whether in race, religion, gender, wealth, or class – as well as in time."

In my view, truly great leaders act from aspirations beyond the goals or boundaries of one organization or group, and rather seek to heal humanity as a whole. I think of Paul Polman, or Bill Gates in the philanthropic phase of his career, or Muhammad Yunus founding the Grameen Bank as exemplars.

These are leaders who grasp the pain of the powerless and of the planet itself, and who seek to repair that damage, whether in ameliorating the diseases that plague the poor, enhancing the viability of local communities, or fighting poverty itself. And the impacts of their strategies will matter far into the future. Wise leaders implicitly follow a dictum that I heard articulated by the Dalai Lama at an MIT conference on global systems. He suggested that when we are making a decision or consider a course of action, we should ask ourselves: Who benefits? Is it just ourselves, or a group? Just one group, or everyone? And just for the present, or also for the future?

These leaders engage people's passion, and foster organizations where work has deeper meaning. Jobs become 'good work,' a powerful combination where people's best skills are engaged fully, their focus fully immersed, and their labor aligned with their values. Such workplaces are potent magnets for the next generation of remarkable leaders.

POSTSCRIPT

Originally Published on LinkedIn.com

ORGANIZATIONAL ATTENTION DEFICIT DISORDER

January 02, 2014

Many leaders in large organizations manage global teams. The group may include contract workers, or team members from a merger. Face-to-face interactions aren't always possible. Getting a group in synch with the project's goals can be a job in and of itself. As a result of these and other obstacles, managers are often forced to operate in good faith that professionals will act accordingly.

But along the way, there are unfortunate breakdowns. Friction arises from constant missed deadlines, miscommunication, or mismanaged budgets. Managers have a hard time comprehending – or responding to – careless errors from professionals. Such breakdowns are a sign of organizational attention deficit.

Ideally people working as a team are going to be attuned to each other. The star performing teams have the highest harmony, and have certain norms for maintaining that harmony, such as:

- They are very aware of each other strengths and weaknesses.
- They let someone step into or out of a role as needed.
- They don't let friction simmer until they explode.
- They deal with it before it becomes a real problem.
- They celebrate wins, and they have a good time together.

This becomes more difficult if people are working at a distance – physically or emotionally. If you have people on a team who don't tune-in, it lowers the harmony. That is exacerbated by a virtual connection, people working by email who never see each other face-to-face.

There are ways to overcome organizational ADD:

- Meet face-to-face. If possible, get everyone together for a one- or two-day offsite meeting. If you know the other person, you can overcome the distance that the virtual world creates.

- Leaders must guide attention. The best leaders sense when and where to shift the collective focus of a team, getting it there at the right time – for example, to capitalize on an emerging trend.

- Set clear project goals. Let people know what's expected, and why their contribution matters in the grand scheme of things.

- Resist the "Us versus Them" mindset. Actively look for the common goal between yourself and the other person or team. This helps eliminate any built-in adversarial filter you bring to a project.

- Provide sufficient time to get the work done. Many managers believe that they can stimulate creativity by putting people under very tight deadlines. That's a myth. In fact, across the board in general, people are more creative when they have a little bit of time to explore a problem, reflect on what they're doing, gather new information, and to talk to people who might have different perspectives, which can be enormously useful.

- Unplug. Tech distractions can affect performance and face-to-face communication. Limit the number of screens open on your computer. Turn off your cell phone if you're under a deadline.

THE ONE LEADERSHIP MUST-HAVE

September 29, 2013

"I like to understand how people see the world," A CEO tells me. "It's always different for each person. I'm fascinated by the ways people think about things, what's important to them, how they put their world together."

That natural curiosity about other people's reality, technically speaking, signifies "cognitive empathy," the ability to see the world through others' eyes. Cognitive empathy is mind-to-mind, giving us a mental sense of how another person's thinking works. It's one of three kinds of empathy, each with a premium in the workplace and in relationships anywhere in our lives.

This way of tuning in to another person does more than give us an understanding of their view – it tells us how best to communicate with that person: what matters most to them, their models of the world, and what even what words to use – or avoid – in talking with them.

And that pays off in many ways. Managers with excellent cognitive empathy, for instance, get better than expected performance from their direct reports. And executives who have this mental asset do well when assigned to a culture different than their own – they are able to pick up the norms and ground rules of another culture more quickly.

But emotional empathy, a second variety, has different benefits. With emotional empathy we feel what the other person does in an instantaneous body-to-body connection. This empathy depends on a different muscle of attention: tuning in to another person's feelings requires we pick up their facial, vocal, and a stream of other nonverbal signs of how they feel instant-to-instant.

This variety of empathy, research shows, depends on our tuning in to our own body's emotional signals, which automatically mirror the other person's feelings.

Daniel Siegel, a UCLA psychiatrist, calls the brain areas that create this resonance the "we" circuitry. Being in the bubble of a "we" with another person can signify chemistry, that sense of rapport that makes whatever we're doing together go well – whether it's in sales or a meeting, in the classroom, or between a couple. Dr. Siegel has even written about how to do this with your teenager.

We see the third variety, empathic concern, spring into action whenever someone expresses their caring about another person. This kind of empathy partakes of the brains' circuitry for parental love – it's a heart-to-heart connection. But it's not out of place at work: you see it when a leader lets people know that he will support them, that she can be trusted, that they are free to take risks rather than maintain a too-safe defensive posture.

In the classroom you see empathic concern when a teacher creates a similar atmosphere and students feel free to let their curiosity roam freely.

Which kind of empathy should a leader, a teacher, or a parent have? All three.

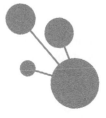

CREDITS

What Makes a Leader?
Originally published in the Harvard Business Review
November/December 1998

Leadership The Gets Results
Originally published in the Harvard Business Review,
March 2000

Primal Leadership: The Hidden Driver of Great Performance
with Richard Boyatzis and Annie McKee. Originally published in the Harvard Business Review, December 2001

Reawkening Your Passion for Work
with Richard Boyatzis and Annie McKee. Originally published in the Harvard Business Review, April 2002

Social Intelligence and the Biology of Leadership
with Richard Boyatzis. Originally published in the Harvard Business Review, September 2008

The Leader's Triple Focus
Adapted from *Focus: The Hidden Driver of Excellence* by Daniel Goleman (2013)

Not Just Smart But Wise – Why Great Leaders Need to Have a Focus Beyond their Organizations
Originally published in Egon Zehnder's *The Focus Magazine*, December 2013